Oklahoma Rough Rider

Oklahoma Rough Rider

Billy McGinty's Own Story

Edited with Commentary and Notes by
Jim Fulbright and Albert Stehno

UNIVERSITY OF OKLAHOMA PRESS : NORMAN

Also by Jim Fulbright
Off and On the Record (Philadelphia, 1972)
The Aviation History of Tennessee (Nashville, 1996)
Aviation in Tennessee: Tennessee's Aviation History in the Stories of People, Places, and Events (Goodlettsville, Tenn., 1998)
Classic Guns of the Old West (Goodlettsville, Tenn., 2000)
W. D. "Bill" Fossett: Pioneer and Peace Officer (Goodlettsville, Tenn., 2002)
Trails to Old Pond Creek: The Early Days of Trade and Travel in Northwestern Oklahoma (Goodlettsville, Tenn., 2005)

This book is published with the generous assistance of the Wallace C. Thompson Endowment Fund, University of Oklahoma Foundation.

Library of Congress Cataloging-in-Publication Data

McGinty, Billy, 1871–1961.
   Oklahoma Rough Rider : Billy McGinty's own story / edited with commentary and notes by Jim Fulbright and Albert Stehno.
       p. cm.
   Includes bibliographical references and index.
   ISBN 978-0-87062-356-1 (hardcover : alk. paper)
   ISBN 978-0-8061-3935-7 (pbk. : alk. paper)
    1. McGinty, Billy, 1871–1961.   2. Spanish-American War, 1898—Personal narratives, American.   3. Cowboys—Oklahoma—Biography.
4. Oklahoma—Biography.   5. Wild west shows.   6. Country music.
I. Fulbright, Jim.   II. Stehno, Albert, 1954–   III. Title.
   CT275.M43417A3 2008
   973.8'9092—dc22
   [B]
                                                              2007049346

The paper in this book meets the guidelines for permanence and durability of the Committee on Production Guidelines for Book Longevity of the Council on Library Resources, Inc. ∞

1 2 3 4 5 6 7 8 9 10

Contents

Illustrations

FIGURES

MAP

Preface

BILLY McGINTY was a tough, wiry little Oklahoma cowboy who volunteered for the Rough Riders and stormed up San Juan Hill with Teddy Roosevelt. By the time he died in 1961 at age ninety, he had accomplished many things in his long life, but none made him as proud as serving with the First United States Volunteer Cavalry in 1898.

In the late 1930s, Billy wrote about his experience as a Rough Rider in what turned out to be one of the rare, firsthand accounts by a front-line soldier. Aside from Roosevelt himself, and professional war correspondents such as Richard Harding Davis, Edward Marshall, and Edwin Emerson (also a Rough Rider), few men recorded a detailed Spanish-American War memoir. That Billy McGinty was an exception is not so surprising, considering his keen sense of history.

Some of his writing was published as part of a local newspaper series titled *The Old West, as Written in the Words of Billy McGinty* (as told to Glenn L. Eyler). The series was issued as a book in a small edition in 1937 and reprinted, again in a small edition, in 1958. Billy's book manuscript "Adventure Trail," which also covered his three years as a performer in Buffalo Bill's Wild West, never made it into print. In 1995 this manuscript was given to us by Delma Imogene Crozier, Billy's granddaughter.

Even though Billy had prepared his text from a distance of nearly forty years, his account faithfully matched known events. For clarity, his narrative required some editing of punctuation and grammar as well as minor reorganizing of chronology. To help provide background and historical perspective, we have occasionally inserted our own commentary by way of italicized notations. Beyond that, Billy's unique personal account speaks for itself, yet it covers only a few years of his adventure-filled life, and much more needed telling. For that reason we added a "Part Two" to his text, our own narrative of his varied careers as a range rider, rancher, bronc buster, and cowboy band promoter—roles that earned him a well-deserved place in the National Cowboy Hall of Fame.

The authors would like to express their gratitude to the following people and organizations whose indispensable help made this book possible: Billy Jay McGinty, Glencoe, Oklahoma; Delma Imogene (McGinty) Crozier, Perry, Oklahoma; Mollie Stehno, Shawnee, Oklahoma; Charles Tingley, Ponca City, Oklahoma; John Dunning, Oklahoma City; Rex Holloway, Arnett, Oklahoma; Chuck Rand, National Cowboy and Western Heritage Museum, Oklahoma City; Linda Gegick, City of Las Vegas, Museum and Rough Rider Memorial Collection, Las Vegas, New Mexico; Loyd Bishop, Ponca City Public Library, Ponca City, Oklahoma; Karen Dye, Newkirk Community Museum, Newkirk, Oklahoma; Towana Spivey, Fort Sill National Historic Landmark and Museum; Oklahoma Historical Society, Oklahoma City; Western History Collections Library, University of Oklahoma, Norman. Finally, our thanks go to copyeditor Jay Fultz for his expert attention to detail and many insightful suggestions for improving the manuscript.

Jim Fulbright
Albert Stehno

Introduction

WILLIAM M. MCGINTY was born in Mercer County, Missouri, on January 1, 1871. Billy was a youngster when his mother died and the family moved to Cowley County, and later, Clark County, Kansas. At age fourteen he stood five feet, four inches, weighed about 130 pounds soaking wet, and never got any bigger. That same year he took a job as a bronc buster at a ranch and stage stop southwest of Dodge City on the Old Mobeetie Trail, a path first carved out by migrating buffalo and Indian hunters before it became a stagecoach, freight, and cattle trail from the Texas Panhandle region. He was a natural at breaking wild horses, and, unlike "many of the boys" who "depended on brute strength to hold tight in the saddle," the diminutive Billy rode, he said, by "feel and balance. It was just like dancing—you got in step with your partner."

In 1887 he drifted into Indian Territory, working as a cowhand with the Comanche Cattle Pool, then on the huge Bar X Bar Ranch in the "Pawnee Triangle" country, west of the confluence of the Cimarron and Arkansas rivers. While there, he first met cowboys-yet-to-turn-outlaws Bill Doolin and George "Bitter Creek" Newcomb.

When "Old Oklahoma" was opened to white settlers on April 22, 1889, Billy helped his father stake a claim southeast of Ingalls. Then he moved west again, working for the A-66 outfit at Pond Creek in the Cherokee Outlet, and then in Texas at cow camps along the Pecos River and Rio Grande. When he returned to Oklahoma Territory during the summer of 1893, he found some of his old cowboy pals from the Bar X Bar Ranch hanging around Ingalls. By then, Bill Doolin and his gang were wanted for bank robbery and other crimes.

In the spring of 1894, Billy struck a trail for New Mexico and Arizona, where he worked on several ranches, ran one himself awhile, and even did a stint as a deputy sheriff in Clifton, Arizona. But in the winter of 1897, his father died, and he returned to Oklahoma to look after his affairs. By then the wide-open West was rapidly changing. The federal census that began the decade showed a clear string of towns and small villages from one end of the country to the other. The frontier was declared officially closed. In Oklahoma alone, there had already been several public land openings with settlers rushing in to occupy millions of acres of farm and pastureland.

Nationwide, the Gay Nineties, as it later became known, was a mixed period of frivolity, business expansion, inventions, immigration, financial panic, and labor strife. People grew more concerned about world events, politics, and the country's future—an awareness that helped move the United States toward its first war in thirty-three years.

Billy was still in Ingalls on February 15, 1898, when a fiery explosion sent the battleship USS *Maine* to the bottom of Havana harbor. The prospect of a war with Spain had loomed for some time with newspapers from eastern cities to the remote regions of the plains carrying vivid stories of Cuban rebellion against Spanish rule. The *Maine*'s sinking fanned anti-Spanish sentiment into a full blaze, and once war was declared, the United States had little difficulty recruiting a volunteer regiment of western cowboys. Billy became one of the first Oklahomans to sign up with the Rough Riders, a role for which he was uniquely qualified.

He helped the regiment break in horses and oversaw their training. He was "tops" as a cowboy and soldier, according to his friend and fellow Rough Rider C. D. Scott of Shawnee, Oklahoma, but when it came to military courtesy, the affable Billy was lacking. He could not distinguish a general from a lieutenant, so he just called them all "boss." Knowing he was a plainspoken man of the range with no formal education, regimental officers were amused, but no one else could have gotten away with the breach of courtesy.

After the war, Billy's cowboy and Rough Rider experience eventually led to a new career. Although the "Wild West" was essentially tamed by 1900, its appeal to the imagination was permanent. In an age of great showmen and traveling entertainers, William Frederick "Buffalo Bill" Cody was most famous. A frontier legend, Cody assembled at various times a remarkable cast of characters for a spectacular Wild West show that included Texas Jack Omohundro, Wild Bill Hickcock, Sitting Bull, and Annie Oakley. Also joining up were scores of frontiersmen, Indians, and cowboys, including Billy and some of his Rough Rider pals. He traveled with Buffalo Bill for three years before returning to Oklahoma to marry and settle down.

In the decades that followed, Billy's natural flair for showmanship and his sense of history were evidenced when he organized the reenactment of Indian raids, cattle drives, and stagecoach robberies during the annual reunions of Oklahoma's "Old Settlers." In the 1920s he helped focus the national spotlight on cowboy music. The "Billy McGinty Cowboy Band" of Ripley, Oklahoma, was a pioneer of western music on live radio, the nation's newest entertainment craze. Another Oklahoma cowboy named Otto Gray, eventually directed the group to even greater fame as the first western band to tour nationally and appear on the cover of *Billboard* Magazine. But it was Billy McGinty who helped organize, manage, and promote the band, taking the initial steps toward popularizing traditional cowboy music, the forerunner of today's country music.

Throughout his life, Billy expressed great pride in his service as a Rough Rider and was devoted to the Rough Riders' Association, an organization formed when the regiment was disbanded in 1898. The veterans held regular reunions to socialize and keep the memory of the First United States Volunteer Cavalry and Theodore Roosevelt alive until all of them were gone. Billy was not the last Rough Rider to pass on, but only a few others outlived him. In their day, they had been the chosen few who, in barely three months during the predawn of the twentieth century, distinguished themselves as one of America's best-remembered volunteer fighting units.

PART I

1898–1901

CHAPTER 1

Into Action with the Rough Riders

IT was early in the year of 1898 that the Spanish sunk the American ship *Maine*. I was at Ingalls, Oklahoma, and had been selling a bunch of horses from Colorado for a man named Bill Laddy, who lived at Colorado Springs. He had been helping me, but left about the first of March to return home, leaving the balance of the horses for me to sell.

The sinking of the *Maine* was the battle cry to war with Spain and Cuban freedom. It was not long after this sinking of the American ship that President McKinley signed the declaration of war. I thought that he should have declared war sooner, but that might have been because I was raring to go down there after those Spaniards.

On February 15, 1898, the American battleship USS Maine, *in Havana harbor, suffered an explosion and quickly sank with the loss of 258 men. Initially, a U.S. court of inquiry determined that a Spanish mine had struck the ship and set off massive explosions in the forward magazines, a conclusion that has been much debated by historians and experts ever since. At the time, however, the American press, led by William Randolph Hearst's* New York Journal *and Joseph Pulitzer's* New York World, *claimed sabotage by the Spaniards and aroused public demands for war with the slogan "Remember the Maine, to hell with Spain." Cuba was already fighting a civil war against Spanish rule, and sympathy for a free Cuba ran high in America. Although President William McKinley was against intervention, the explosion of the USS* Maine *crystallized public opinion, and on April 25, Congress declared war.*[1]

One of the reasons I wanted to go so bad was that a friend of mine in Arizona named "Sansimo Jack" had gone down in 1896 to aid the Cubans in their fight from Spanish slavery. He had told me of the cruelties heaped on the Cubans in their own land, and from his words it was simply terrible. "Sansimo Jack" with many other soldiers had their way paid to Cuba, although the U.S. government was not actually at war with Spain at that time.

My father had passed away in the winter of 1897, and I had no binding ties left. I thought that the place for me was to follow the trail of adventure wherever it might lead, and the news of forming the Rough Riders greatly appealed to me. I had only two problems, one to find a place to pasture my horses, and the other to find where to enlist.

I went up to Stillwater, Oklahoma, and was directed to see Robert Lowry. He was a lawyer and one of the early-day civic leaders for our county. He told me that nine men would be selected from every county in Oklahoma Territory, and he put me down as one of the nine men from Payne County. The board members who made the selections picked leaders from each county, and Mr. Lowry told me that he would keep me posted when and where to go to enlist.

Influential Stillwater attorney Robert Lowry commanded Company L of the First Territorial Volunteer Infantry that trained at Fort Reno, Oklahoma Territory. It was part of a second wave of volunteer units mobilized for the Spanish-American War.[2]

Troops, A, B, and C were comprised of Arizona Militia assembled at Prescott. Troop D was organized in Oklahoma. Troops E, F, G, and H were the New Mexico Militia organized at Santa Fe. Troop I was organized at San Antonio from transfers of other troops and its membership comprised twenty-three states of the Union. Troop K contained men from northern states organized at Washington, D.C., as well as transfers of men from Troop D and E. Troop L and M were organized at Muskogee, Indian Territory. [All] these troops made up the First United States Volunteer Cavalry, popularly known as the Rough Riders. Their record of organization, marches, battles, and other achievement during their brief period of enlistment has no equal in military history or warfare.

The Rough Riders were made up of men who were ready, who knew the use of horse and gun, who were healthy and weather-toughened. It was necessary that a large number of troops be ready in a short amount of time. So it was that these men from the plains and the hill country—cowboys, miners, hunters, and sportsmen—all came together for instant service.

The First U.S. Volunteer Cavalry became known as "Rough Riders" after the regiment was formed. Theodore Roosevelt, assistant secretary of navy under President McKinley, had long advocated war with Spain, as did Dr. Leonard Wood, the president's medical advisor and a veteran of Indian campaigns in the Southwest. Roosevelt and Wood's like-mindedness did not escape the president who, in the days following the USS Maine's explosion, asked Wood, "Have you and Theodore declared war yet?" Wood did not mind the joke and answered, "No, Mr. President, but we think you should."

Both men requested commissions when Congress authorized the raising of "three cavalry regiments from among the wild riders and riflemen of the Rockies and the Great Plains." Roosevelt was offered a regiment but, considering his own lack of military experience, asked to serve as second-in-command under Wood, a request that was approved by the president and secretary of war. The public soon dubbed the First U.S. Volunteer Cavalry the "Rough Riders," a term Wood and Roosevelt at first disliked, until the press and even the army brass began using it. The unit was to consist of volunteers from the territories of New Mexico, Arizona, Oklahoma, and Indian Territory. The problem lay not in accepting but in rejecting the overwhelming number of applicants for the 780 positions available. When the quota was raised to 1,000, Wood and Roosevelt began accepting a number of highly qualified volunteers from the states,

Billy McGinty (second from right, holding the horse down) oversees the shoeing of a Rough Rider mount at San Antonio, teaching fellow troopers a much faster method of putting four shoes on at one time. Courtesy of CSCPA Collection.

making for a truly diverse unit ranging from Ivy League college men to cowboys.

The Second and Third Volunteer Cavalry units, primarily made up of cowboys from the northern plains and other western states, never shipped out to Cuba and were disbanded later in the year.[3]

After returning to Ingalls, I went over into Indian Territory to find a place to pasture my horses. When I got back, there was a letter telling me to report in at Guthrie on April 29, which was the next day. I spent the afternoon and evening in one mad rush to get someone to look after the rest of my things, and it was one [ten?] o'clock on April 28 before I got away.

The forepart of the night was light until about three o'clock, and then it seemed so dark it made the traveling very hard. It was about a forty-five-mile ride down to Guthrie. I had crossed the Cimarron River before the moon went down, and after that, I was not quite sure of my directions, but kept on what I thought was a southwesterly course.

At that time of night, I could see no lights in any of the farmhouses, as most people went to bed at the same time the chickens roosted, leaving little chance for me to find out if I was on the right trail. I kept on riding, and about an hour or so before daylight, I saw a light down a draw some distance away. I rode down this draw and came upon a cabin. An old darky man and woman came to the door, and I asked them how far it was to Guthrie. They said that it was about sixteen miles. I told them what I was aiming to do, and asked them if I could come in and lie down by their fireplace for a while. They told me I was surely welcome, so I got down and slept for a time. Shortly after daybreak, the old couple woke me, gave me some bread and coffee, and I started off again.

I hurried on to Guthrie and arrived in plenty of time, so I put my pony in a livery stable, and later that morning sold him to a man named Wheeler. In Guthrie I ran across several of the boys I knew, and they told me that the head officer, who would muster us in, would not arrive until the next day. We were billeted at a hotel there and there was a honky-tonk nearby. The boys nearly took that honky-tonk apart that night and sure "raised Cain."

The next morning, Captain [Allyn] Capron, later of Troop L, Rough Riders, arrived and we were all ordered to undergo an examination in a building close to where the Ione Hotel now stands. Not all the boys examined passed. I believe that I was the only man from Payne County who was accepted. Some were turned down because of size; they were too big and heavy for cavalrymen.

Boy-e-e, I sure was feeling good when they told me I had passed. We all lined up to be mustered in and the commanding officer asked that anyone who felt like they should not go, to step back two paces. The entire line held.

The formal mustering, or swearing-in, of Oklahoma's volunteers occurred in the territorial capital of Guthrie on May 7, with twenty-six-

year-old career officer Captain Allyn Capron presiding. The Brooklyn, New York, native had joined the army in 1890 and had recently served with the Seventh Cavalry at Fort Sill. Four years earlier, he had supervised the transfer of Geronimo and his Apache band from an Alabama prison camp to Fort Sill. After Capron volunteered for the Rough Riders, Colonel Leonard Wood named him regimental adjutant with orders to recruit Oklahomans.

As Capron called roll, each volunteer answered by taking two steps forward. The territorial governor Cassius Barnes witnessed the mass swearing-in, then gave a rousing speech to the new soldiers. The ceremony included the presentation of a thoroughbred horse to Troop D commanding officer Captain Robert Bell Huston, a thirty-four-year-old Guthrie attorney. The ambitious Huston, a captain in the Oklahoma National Guard, craved a military career, telling his wife, "This is my opportunity, and I'm not wearing out the seat of my trousers sitting around." He went on to serve in the Philippines after Cuba, but died there of typhoid fever.[4]

A week later, on May 14, 1898, Captain Capron swore in the Indian Territory recruits at Muskogee. They had been recruited by Judge John R. Thomas, a former Civil War Union Army officer serving as special judge for Indian Territory. Judge Thomas acted on War Department orders to enlist "175 picked men, good shots and good riders," as part of a volunteer cavalry regiment. In less than two weeks he organized two hundred men into Troops L and M of the Rough Riders. The men who passed the judge's screening and a doctor's medical exam had to sleep on hay upstairs in Muskogee's Women's Christian Temperance Union building, where they were besieged by mosquitos. On one warm night, a sentry demanded to know why a young recruit had come downstairs carrying a handful of hay. The recruit replied that he was "moving his bed downstairs."[5]

Before the volunteers departed by rail for their San Antonio, Texas, training site, Captain Capron was appointed commanding officer for Rough Rider Troop L, and Judge Thomas's son, John R., Jr., was commissioned a first lieutenant.[6] The men assigned to Indian Territory's Troop M, as it turned out, would never make it to Cuba. They remained, instead, at the Tampa, Florida, embarkation point with three other Rough

Captain Allyn K. Capron, a fifth-generation soldier stationed with the Seventh Cavalry at Fort Sill, was appointed regimental adjutant and charged with recruiting Oklahoma and Indian Territory volunteers when the war began. Courtesy of the Fort Sill National Historic Landmark and Museum.

Rider troops, caring for the horses and many supplies that could not be loaded on the overcrowded transports.[7]

We [Oklahoma Territory's volunteers] marched down to the train that stood ready to take us to San Antonio but when we started boarding, we found the coaches locked. The officers went after the conductor to open up, but when they got back, the boys were already on the train. They had broken the windows and crawled in. Nothing was said about which ones broke the glass for fear they would court-martial us all.

Us bunch of yokels had a good time on that trip and when we reached the station at San Antonio we unloaded at the fairgrounds southeast of town. There were a few troops already

there but Colonel [Leonard] Wood, and Lieutenant Colonel
Roosevelt did not arrive until a few days later.

I was mustered into D Troop, but when Roosevelt and Wood
got there, they started changing things around. Some troops
had too many men; others did not have enough, so I went from
D to K Troop. Now, K Troop, as I mentioned, was made up of
men from the north and east; of hunters, polo players, and rich
men's sons. Many of them had traveled all over the world and
had joined the trail of adventure to find more thrills in their
lives. This kind of business appealed to them and they wanted
to be toughened to hardships. They were mighty fine fellows,
every one of them. I first thought I would not like them, but I
found out that they were real men, plenty willing to do their
part any time and anywhere. Their courage and perseverance
have made many of them, such as Goodrich, Knoblauck, and
Knox, world figures.

*Lieutenant David M. Goodrich, captain of the Harvard rowing crew
and considered by Roosevelt to be one of the country's "most noted college
athletes," eventually followed his father's lead in the rubber industry,
establishing the nation's automobile tire industry and serving as CEO of
B. F. Goodrich for nearly four decades. The Knoblauck brothers, George
and Charles, became members of the New York Stock Exchange, and
William Franklin Knox would be secretary of war during most of World
War Two. Although not all of them were from New York, these eastern
men who rushed to join the regiment when the initial quota was increased
were dubbed the "Fifth Avenue Boys."[8]*

After my transfer to K Troop, we began getting our horses.
We would ride over to Fort Sam Houston, which was about
four miles from the fairgrounds and our camp. The horses were
small and none too gentle.

By this time, many more troops began pouring into the
camp, and sometimes we'd go down to the cars to see if we
knew any of them. I ran across several of the boys I knew from
Arizona and other points of the West.

Five of the regiment's bronc busters at the San Antonio training site. Left to right: Billy McGinty, Troop K; Morris J. Storms, Troop I; Roscoe E. Moore, Troop I; William D. Wood, Troop G; Sergeant Thomas Darnell, Troop H. Courtesy of Bartleby.com, Inc. © 1997.

The horses that we picked up at the fort were just regular south Texas and Mexico horses and they all had to be shod before we left for Cuba. Because Cuba was very mountainous, they told us that we should get the horses shod at once. No one in K Troop knew much about shoeing horses, because I watched them for a time and saw it was working into a big job for them. I had not been detailed for it, but had worked with horses quite a bit, and after watching their progress, I went to our captain, Woodbury Kane, and told him that if the boys would throw the horses and tie them down, the job would be much easier.

The captain didn't pay me any mind, and as I didn't know any of the other officers, I said nothing more to the captain. I told one of the boys to let me show him how to do the job. I had shoed many a wild bronco and knew how to handle them.

I put the rope on the horse's front feet and threw him to the ground. Then I tied the horse above his hocks and above his front knees, and put a leg on each side of him, so that his legs were crossed and sticking straight up in the air. That way more men could help shoe the horse at the same time and get the job done real fast.

Colonel Roosevelt and Lieutenant [Horace K.] Devereaux were at headquarters near where the boys were working. They came over to see what was going on and I sure thought that I would get a bawling out. I knew Lieutenant Devereaux, and he introduced me to the colonel. Roosevelt knew the West and the work of a cowboy. He watched for a while and remarked that the horses were being shod in such a short time saying, "That is bully!" That word "bully" was his most common expression of pleasure, and many times I've heard him compliment the boys of the Rough Riders with, "Young man, that was bully work!"

By this time, McGinty and a few other veteran bronc busters were excused from daily drill because of their expertise at breaking horses. Billy had already been reproved for his inability to keep step during drill because of his short legs, but responded that he was "pretty sure he could keep step on horseback." Regimental officers described him as "an amazing character from Stillwater, Oklahoma," standing only five feet, five inches with blue eyes and sandy hair, and looking much younger than his twenty-seven years. He seemed "glued to the back of bucking broncos" and "could ride any horse that came along." Roosevelt remarked of him: "We had no braver or better man in the fights."[9]

A regiment in those days contained about 1,200 men, and we had 1,295 horses in our outfit. Each man had his equipment and had to carry an extra shoe in the saddle pocket. They were numbered one, two, or three, according to size and were called "ready-to-fit" shoes. After getting our horses shod we drilled on horseback, but the ground was so dusty that a big cloud of dust was about all that could be seen. We tried drilling at the fairgrounds but didn't get much good out of it. Some of the horses we had were plenty mean, and one of the boys in our regiment was killed while drilling when his horse threw him against a tree.

The commissioned officers had to furnish their own horses and saddles, so the Texas ranchers and cowboys would bring in some prize horses to sell to the officers. Lieutenant [Micah John] Jenkins asked me to keep my eye out for a good mount for him. Jenkins was an early-day soldier, having been stationed at Fort Supply in Indian Territory. Several of the boys knew him as a great soldier and a fine man. I found him a good horse and bought it for him. Later, when the war was over, and we were mustered out at Montauk Point, Lieutenant Jenkins, who had been made a major on the battlefield, gave this horse to me.

Micah John Jenkins, a South Carolinian, graduated from West Point in 1879. Roosevelt said that he was a man "on whom danger acted like wine, a perfect gamecock, and he won his majority for gallantry in battle."[10]

We stayed at San Antonio until May 28 and then loaded up on trains for Tampa, Florida. We arrived at Tampa on June 3 and unloaded on a big sandy flat that had trees with no branches for about thirty feet up from the ground. We marched down to a hotel over some of the hottest sand that I ever walked on. There, they handed us our first paycheck, which for most of us boys amounted to thirteen dollars. Those of us who had been working for cow outfits had made more money than that, but it made no difference because we all wanted to go to Cuba.

When we got back to camp from payday, the word got around that the transports could carry only a few troops and none of the horses. We were all raring to go, but the thought of having to stay in camp and do camp duty and not go straight to the front made many of the boys grouchy.

Everybody got to wondering who would get to go first. I thought that since I had been transferred to K Troop, I would have to wait awhile, and was feeling sorry that I had been transferred, because D Troop was slated to go first. The talk was that the other troops and horses would follow in a short time, but everybody wanted to board the first boat.

I wanted to go on that first boat, too, and as I was walking down the company streets between the dog tents, I saw Colonel Teddy Roosevelt a short distance away, so I hailed him and asked him if Troop K would go on the first boat. He replied, "Don't worry McGinty; you'll go on the first boat." I went back to our mess tent and heard some of the boys talking and they said Troop K would be left behind. That had me worried some, for I just couldn't figure out how I would go and the troop be left behind, so I just figured that I'd remind Colonel Roosevelt of his promise before the first troops left.

There were five days of this sort of indecision, and on June 8, when things finally got worked out, Troop K was a happy bunch when orders came that they were to go on the first boat. We all boarded flat cars and went down to Tampa Bay, which was about five miles from camp, and marched aboard a former cattle boat called the *Yucatan.*

This old boat had been fixed up with bunks of straw that were boxed up for two in a bed. When we boarded, orders were to stay aboard. Some officers from other outfits came aboard and told us that the boat had been assigned to them and that we would have to get off, but it would have taken a large army to move us. They finally ran the *Yucatan* out in the bay and we anchored until the other boats were ready.

There was tremendous disarray at Port Tampa, and the Fifth Corps, of which the Rough Riders were a part, was highly disorganized. The rail line leading into the port had only one set of tracks, forcing freight cars with provisions, medicines, and materials to back up for miles. Because invoices and bills of lading had been misplaced, the army was compelled to break the locks and seals on over three hundred cars just to determine what they contained. As the humid Florida weather reached 110 degrees,

Transport number eight, the *Yucatan*, crammed with soldiers both above and below decks, prepares to steam out of Port Tampa for Cuba with 578 enlisted Rough Riders, about half the regiment, along with four companies of the Second Regular Infantry. Courtesy of Bartleby.com, Inc. © 1997.

most of the troopers suffered in their winter woolen uniforms because the lightweight ones were sitting on a sidetrack twenty-five miles from port. A Chicago newspaper reporter wrote of the chaos: "I have seen sights at dock and railheads unmatched except in some huge lunatic asylum."

To make matters worse, the commercial transports dispatched to take the army to Cuba were capable of carrying only about two-thirds of the troops. In the confusion, several regiments were assigned to the transport Yucatan, an enormous, filthy, commercial steamer. Although the Seventy-first New York Infantry was among the units designated to board the Yucatan, Colonel Leonard Wood realized early on that the fleet was short of space. He rushed to get 33 Rough Rider officers and 578 enlisted men on board, knowing that, once on, they could probably not be forced off. The Rough Riders stayed on, to the chagrin of other regiments.

Next, in one of the worst bureaucratic blunders of the war, the invasion fleet of twenty-one transports and fourteen warships was delayed in Tampa harbor by a false rumor of lurking Spanish warships. Seventeen thousand men sweltered on iron ships, without fresh food or ice, for a week. Their anchorage was described as a "sea of sewage." On June 14, *the fleet finally departed, and because of the shortage of transports, only eight of twelve Rough Rider troops went to Cuba. Troops C, H, I, and M remained in Florida. The regiment also left the horses and the troopers' revolvers behind. In Cuba, the Rough Riders essentially served as an infantry regiment.*[11]

We were on board for six days before sailing, and finally on June 14, we started for Cuba with thirty-five vessels all lined up, four abreast, steaming out to sea. This was some sight and one of the finest of my recollection. At night when the ships were all lit up, it looked like a small town; with lights forming a village built on a hill because the ships ahead of us seemed to be higher than the others.

We had been out to sea only a few days when the *Yucatan* came near burning up. Some one had lit a cigarette and caught his bunk afire, and with the windows open the whole deck was filled with smoke. It was finally put out but it gave me a scary feeling to think the ship was afire.

At one point the ships suddenly all came to a stop. The front ships had sighted a vessel in the distance and the gunboats went on ahead to see if it was an enemy ship. It was only a South American ship, so we continued. As we neared Cuba, orders came for the *Yucatan* to stick close by the armored cruiser USS *New York,* which was listing and in danger of sinking, but it made it all right. If it had sunk, I don't see how we could have taken any more aboard. We were carrying fifteen hundred men and it looked pretty well loaded to me.

We were on the way for eight days, and during that time it was necessary to get a little washing done. There was no laundryman, and I noticed some of the boys tying their clothes to a rope and letting them drag astern. This seemed to beat the dirt out of them and they looked pretty good, so I thought I would try it. I took my pants, tied them to a rope, and threw them out in the ocean. I let them float along in the salt water and went on about my business. I forgot about them for quite a while, and when I went to pull them in, they were clean all right, but nearly worn to threads. I wore them for a few days, but they finally came all to pieces. The captain had an old pair of cockney pants he gave me. They were a few sizes too big, but that didn't matter since I had pants again, and I wore them the rest of the time.

The first sight of Santiago was impressive. We dropped anchor about ten or twelve miles out from the bay. The town sets back from the mouth of the bay about two or three miles. At one point, just across from the Morro Castle, which stands about 800 feet above the sea, the bay is barely wide enough for one ship to pass another.

Santiago, on Cuba's southeast shore, west of Guantánamo Bay, was founded by conquistadors in 1514 and was the second most important city in Cuba after Havana. Castles on promontories, or morros, were built in both Havana and Santiago harbors about 1589 to protect the cities from buccaneers. They served as fortresses, lookout points, and prisons.[12]

It was just as the sun was coming up when we neared the bay, and I could see a great mass of smoke curling up from back in the mountains. I could not see the town, but it seemed like jets of smoke from hundreds of chimneys fleeted skyward to form a great mass in the early morning quietness as the townspeople arose to get their morning meal. Santiago's population was then about one hundred thousand, and I will long remember seeing it for the first time.

About ten o'clock that morning there came a strong undercurrent [riptide], the first I was ever in, and it seemed to me that the boat would turn over any minute. The ship flopped from one side to the other and most of us couldn't keep our feet, so we just crawled around. The officers had big, heavy teacups and saucers in their cabins and the ship's pitching about bounced them around all over the room. They were so big that if one happened to hit you, it certainly could be felt. This heavy sea lasted for about six hours, and I, for one, was certainly glad to get out of it.

By this time, Admiral William Sampson had already blockaded Santiago harbor with U.S. warships, trapping the Spanish flotilla inside. Moving closer posed a problem because enemy shore batteries and deadly mines protected the harbor. Sampson wanted Major General William Rufus Shafter, commanding the Fifth Corps, to land his army and dismantle these fortifications, thus allowing the navy to enter the harbor, remove the mines, and then proceed to the city. Shafter saw this as a tactic that would leave the deadliest work to his ground forces while the navy swept in to take the city and capture the glory.

On the afternoon of June 20, General Shafter and Admiral Sampson met with Cuban General Calixto García. As a result of this consultation, it was determined to land the first American soldiers about fifteen miles east of Santiago at the small village of Daiquiri.[13]

On the morning of June 22, the Rough Riders and other troops landed at Daiquiri, Cuba. The order was surely welcome, for the sea had been a bit wallowy. Daiquiri was a mining town, not very large, and we had to anchor about three miles out for fear of taking the big boats any closer. We went ashore in rowboats, and it was a mad scramble as each officer had command of the unloading. Our small gunboats fired at the enemy on shore so they would not know our exact landing spot.

There was no dock at Daiquiri and with the tide coming in, the shore looked like a big bank of snow. The breakers topped out at fifteen to twenty feet high, and on the hillsides beyond we could see each shell exploding. There was a prison camp here, and we found out later that the Spanish left it with the prisoners still inside when the shelling began. The Cuban prisoners took refuge in the big iron baking ovens to escape the shelling while we came ashore.

The only horses on the transports were those belonging to the officers, and as we launched the rowboats with the men in them, the horses were brought up on deck. We had no way to get them ashore, but they helped themselves on that question. After being cooped up in the hole of the hot ship for so long, they jumped in the water and began swimming for land. A few headed the wrong way, and went out to sea and were drowned. Several of the officers lost some good horses this way, including Colonel Roosevelt, who lost one of his.

The landing at Daiquiri was some job. The small rowboats came alongside the transport and when the big waves brought the smaller boats up higher in the water, the boys would jump off and into them. Once loaded, they would head toward shore.

A short distance off shore from the little town was a pen built of logs that was anchored down. When the tide got high enough, the boys would jump out on these logs. When it came my time to jump, I threw my bedding over the side on to what I thought was a platform on the other side of the logs. It hit right into the water. I got it back but it was sure soaking wet. When I finally got on shore, I had a hard time walking for a while. It seemed as though I needed to brace myself to just stand up, and I found out right then what was meant by "sailor's legs."

The landing at Daiquiri, like everything that preceded it, was marred by confusion. Roosevelt called it a "scramble." The navy had less than a quarter of the small boats necessary for landing the thousands of soldiers it transported, and once launched, the boats bobbed like corks in the heaving seas, sometimes smashing to kindling against the offshore pilings. The process consumed the entire day and much of the night. Partial blame for the landing debacle lay in the refusal of transport captains to bring their vessels in close to shore. News correspondent Richard Harding Davis wrote in Scribner's *magazine: "Transport captains acted with independence and disregard of what was expected of them. For the greater part of each day they kept from three to twenty miles out to sea, where it was impossible to communicate with them."*

The "pen built of logs" that McGinty refers to was an abandoned boat dock. A landing craft carrying troopers from the Tenth Cavalry hit

the pilings, sending two "buffalo soldiers" [African-Americans] bur-
dened with heavy packs straight to the bottom. William O. "Buckey"
O'Neill, captain of Arizona's Rough Rider Troop A, dived in, fully
clothed, in a heroic attempt to save them, but found no trace of either
man. They apparently sank to the bottom under the weight of cartridge
belts, packs, and bedrolls. About the only positive aspect of the landing
at Daiquiri was the absence of the enemy. Although the Spaniards had
an estimated 36,000 soldiers in and around Santiago, the Americans
were unopposed.[14]

After the boys were all unloaded, we went out to a cocoanut
grove close to the town and made camp, then returned to look
around. Some of the officers were rolling out barrels of rum
and knocking out the heads of the barrels and letting it run
down the street. The streets were gravelly, some kind of sand,
and a few of the soldiers went along and used tin cups to dip
up rum from the little grooves where it had run, and fill their
canteens.

After roaming around awhile, we returned to camp and then
got orders to be ready to march at any time. It wasn't very long
before we moved out, starting off over the mountains with only
a small trail to follow under dark, rainy skies. We had to stay on
this trail and blunder along the best we could because of the
dense underbrush on all sides of us. We kept track of our direction by the high-powered lights of the ships on the ocean. Several officers rode along to help the way to our destination,
which was a place called Siboney. We were like a bunch of cattle in a trail herd headed for water, but I would have felt better
on the bed ground.

When we got close to Siboney it was nearing daylight. Everything was lit up because the forces ahead of us had built a big
fire. I asked a fellow where I could get a drink of water and he
told me that a short distance away was a big spring. I went
down to get me a drink and as I reached over to dip a tin cup
full, I slipped and fell into the water. The spring was about three

feet wide and it came up to right under my arms. It felt so good, that I just stood there and drank my fill of water.

We went on into town. The Spanish had already been driven off and our forces occupied it. One of the Cuban soldiers stationed there interested me very much. He was just a trooper, dressed only in a breechcloth, and looked real young for a soldier. I went over and talked with him, and he told me he was all of twelve years old. There were other Cuban soldiers that didn't look much older than he did.

We got something to eat and about eight o'clock in the morning started up the mountain on a narrow trail that was just a wagon road. On both sides of us was heavy timber, mostly mahogany and some coconut trees. As we neared the front, we had our advance guard out.

The plan called for General Shafter's Fifth Corps to move westward from Daiquiri and encircle the port and town of Santiago. Brigadier General Henry Ware Lawton, a Civil War Medal of Honor winner, had already marched ahead with the Second Infantry Division to secure Siboney, which was about midway between Daiquiri and Santiago.

Meanwhile, sixty-two-year-old General Joe Wheeler, also a Civil War veteran, but for the Confederacy, followed close behind with his dismounted cavalry division. "Fightin' Joe" Wheeler had been under fire in an estimated eight hundred skirmishes and battles during his campaigns from Shiloh to Chickamauga. He had harassed Sherman's army in their march to Atlanta, and although rather frail-looking, he was still gutsy and aggressive. Wheeler commanded the Fifth Corps' cavalry division, composed of two brigades. The First Brigade included the Third, Sixth, and Ninth Cavalry regiments under Brigadier General S. S. Sumner; and the Second Brigade contained the First and the Tenth Regular Cavalry, as well as the First U.S. Volunteer Cavalry–Rough Riders–under Brigadier General S. B. M. Young. Wheeler's job was to join General Lawton's lead forces and then position his troops as part of a two-pronged attack on Santiago, but while Lawton set up his defenses at Siboney, Wheeler pushed on toward Las Guasimas with his dismounted cavalry division. On the morning of June 24, his troops fought the first land engagement in the Santiago campaign.[15]

Tom Isbell, a part-Cherokee Indian, was one of the advance guards of L Troop, and when the shooting started, some Spanish soldiers began firing at him. Tom and the enemy fired at close range and as soon as he killed one of them, it seemed like the entire Spanish Army opened fire on him at once. After he had been shot seven times, the last bullet taking him off his feet, he raised upon his elbow, looked over toward the enemy lines and said, "You know I think some one over there is shooting at me." Tom bled a lot, and doctors said they thought this helped save his life. He now resides in southern California.

The twenty-three-year-old Isbell, from Vinita, Oklahoma, fired the Rough Riders' first shot of the land war at Las Guasimas. Other members of Troop L who would distinguish themselves in the days ahead included forty-year-old Cherokee Indian John Martin Adair of Fort Gibson, a first cousin to Oklahoma's Will Rogers;[16] *twenty-seven-year-old Second Lieutenant Richard Cushing Day of Vinita, who refused to stay in a field hospital after being wounded at San Juan Hill;*[17] *and twenty-two-year-old college student Thomas F. Meagher of Muskogee, the trumpeter for L Troop and the grandson of General Thomas F. Meagher, of the famed "Irish Brigade" in the Civil War.*[18]

We had eight or nine killed in this skirmish, which was a part of the Battle of Las Guasimas, and happened on June 24, 1898. The Spanish Army was in a "V" shape, and we were headed for the center of this "V." The Rough Riders deployed to each side, facing the point of the "V." One side was rather rocky and the Spanish had taken to these rocks and hidden.

We had two rapid-fire guns, including parts that were packed on two mules. When the firing started one of the mules broke loose and started back down the mountains, so we had no rapid-fire guns. While the firing was going on pretty heavy,

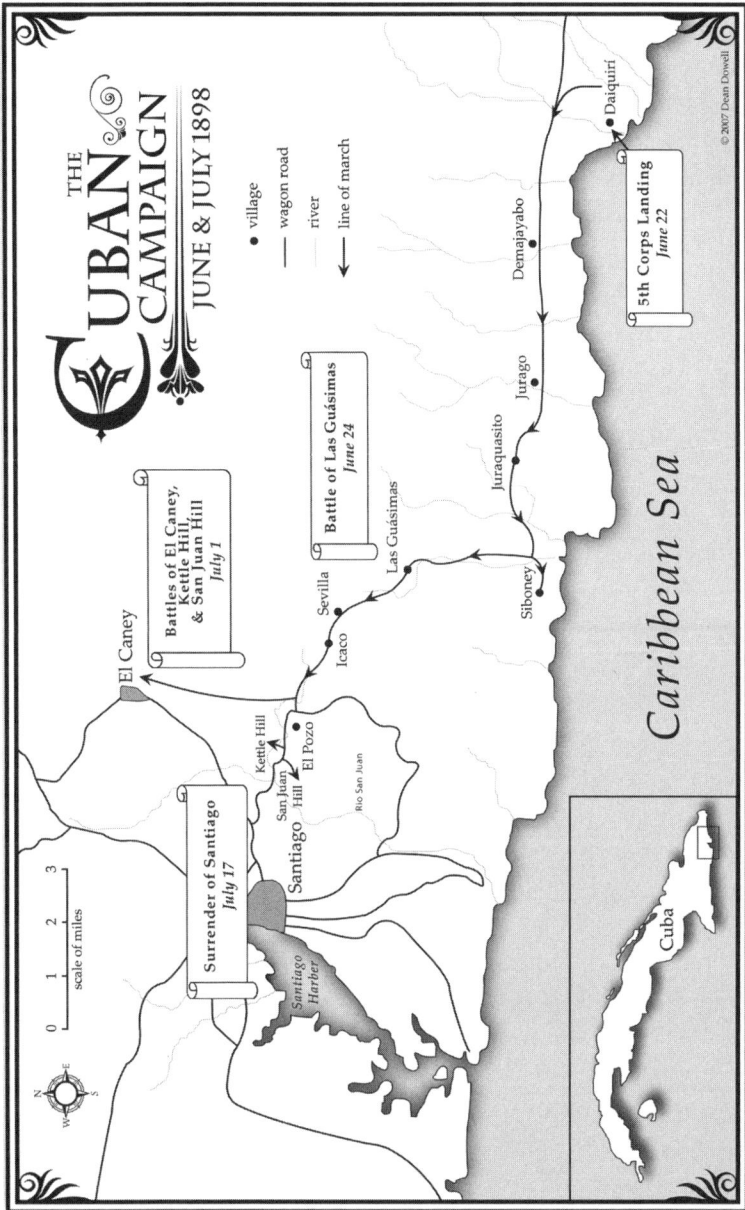

THE CUBAN CAMPAIGN
JUNE & JULY 1898

• village
— wagon road
— river
→ line of march

© 2007 Dean Dowell

Daiquiri

Demajayabo

5th Corps Landing
June 22

Jurago

Juraquasito

Battle of Las Guásimas
June 24

Las Guásimas

Siboney

Sevilla

Icaco

Battles of El Caney,
Kettle Hill,
& San Juan Hill
July 1

El Caney

Kettle Hill

El Pozo

San Juan
Hill

Rio San Juan

Santiago

Surrender of Santiago
July 17

Santiago
Harbor

Caribbean Sea

Cuba

N
W   E
S

0   1   2   3
scale of miles

23

Lieutenant Colonel Roosevelt and Colonel Wood rode up on an open glade for a talk to plan further action. They were under heavy fire, but they just sat and talked for what seemed to me a long time. We had taken to cover, and I was at the base of a hill and kept wondering why they didn't come down. Then Roosevelt and Wood split up and orders came to advance, and they led the troopers up against the Spanish. We routed them and they retreated toward Santiago, taking as many of their dead and wounded as possible.

At Las Guasimas, Wheeler's troops ran into the rear guard of the retiring Spanish force. Wheeler directed General Young's Second Brigade, with the Rough Riders, to make the initial strike. The battle opened with a volley from American Hotchkiss guns, and was quickly answered by a withering barrage of fire from nearly fifteen hundred expertly camouflaged enemy soldiers who were entrenched in the hills north of Siboney.

Colonel Wood and Lieutenant Colonel Roosevelt urged the foot-weary Rough Riders forward as enemy fire erupted all around them. As McGinty has noted, Tom Isbell, a redheaded Oklahoma cowboy, was among the first to taste enemy fire. Peering through some brush, Isbell found a Spaniard in his Krag rifle sights and pulled the trigger. The enemy soldier instantly fell, setting off a fusillade of Mauser bullets, all aimed at Isbell. The intrepid Isbell returned fire, eventually receiving seven gunshot wounds in the skirmish. Refusing medical attention and bleeding profusely, he remained in the battle until so weakened by blood loss that he had to be carried back to Siboney.

Heading the advance with Isbell was Sergeant Hamilton Fish of New York. The grandson and namesake of the secretary of state under President Ulysses S. Grant, and former captain of the Columbia University rowing crew, he was fatally struck in the chest by an enemy bullet. It passed through his body and hit Private Ed Culver of Muskogee under the left arm.

A few minutes later, Captain Allyn Capron, a fifth-generation army volunteer, considered by Roosevelt as the "best soldier in the regiment," also fell to enemy fire. Capron took a painful hour to die, the first U.S.

Army officer killed in the Spanish-American War. With his death, the command of L Troop passed to Lieutenant John R. Thomas of Muskogee, Oklahoma, but the severity of a leg wound, suffered in the same firefight, put Thomas out of action, transferring command to Second Lieutenant Richard C. Day of Vinita, Oklahoma.

By midafternoon, the enemy firing slowly tapered off as the Spanish withdrew. The Rough Riders and other Fifth Corps troops finally built camp, staking their claim to the heights east of San Juan Hill and Santiago. Rough Rider losses at Las Guasimas were eight dead and thirty-four wounded. Roosevelt gave special commendation to the many Oklahoma troopers in this battle, including Tom Isbell, whom he singled out for "conspicuous gallantry."[19]

We had very little to eat, and after the fight we found several Spanish Army pack mules that had been shot. They were loaded with packs of beans, but we got orders not to eat any of them for they might be poisoned. We found a batch of chickens staked out near their trenches, but I never got any of them. Some of the dead Spaniards left on the field had their packs full of Cuban cigars, so some of the boys got a smoke.

We went into camp there and stayed that night. I had thrown my dog tent away because it was too heavy to carry and had split my blanket to make my pack lighter. Captain [Woodbury] Kane asked me what I had done with my dog tent, and I told him that I had thrown it away. He told me to lay down my blanket, and he laid his down, and we pulled the half of tent he had over us and slept very well that night. The next morning we all felt like eating something but didn't have much food.

We began marching down an old wagon road until finally given orders to fall out and rest. A Massachusetts regiment came marching by, and each man was carrying an extra half gallon of tomatoes. They saw we had only a little hardtack to eat so they brought out their tomatoes and we had a feast.

We followed on down this road with a big high mountain to our right and finally went into camp for the night by a small creek. Some of the boys had a few chocolate bars and we whittled these up and fared pretty well. There were a large number of San Juan Hill [fruit] trees around and they were ripe. They are about as big as an average orange and looked somewhat like a small squash. They are rather stringy eating, but taste kind of good if they are cooked with sugar. The Cubans lived on these and coconuts.

The San Juan Hill trees have large leaves, making it nearly impossible to see a man hiding in them. The enemy would tie bunches of these leaves about their body and hide in those trees. Many of the Spanish sharpshooters hid in them and our army could pass right by and never see them. I never cared much for hunting out these sharpshooters because they had the advantage of seeing you when you couldn't see them. The only way to get them was to fire volley after volley into the trees and that would have been a lifetime job [because] there were so many of them.

It is unclear what McGinty means by "San Juan Hill tree." It may have been a nickname soldiers gave to one of the native tropical fruit trees.

The Rough Riders and other troops received a six-day respite following the Las Guasimas battle, camping near Siboney before continuing the drive to take Santiago. In the meantime, more troops and material landed on the Siboney beach while the wounded were moved on to hospital transports. During this period, General Young developed a fever, and Colonel Leonard Wood was promoted to brigadier general, assuming command of the entire Second Brigade (First Regular and Tenth Colored cavalries, along with the Rough Riders). Theodore Roosevelt was promoted to full colonel, taking command of the Rough Riders.[20]

CHAPTER 2

The Push to Santiago
and San Juan Hill

FIVE miles east of Santiago, on the line of march, lay El Pozo Hill (some-times El Poso), a vantage point General Shafter's officers had used to watch enemy movements for several days. They could also see the ridges and rivers between there and Santiago, including the San Juan Heights, a series of hills dominated by several fortified positions known as block-houses. The Rough Riders and other troops made camp close to El Pozo Hill the night of June 30 to await the next day's battle.

To take Santiago, Shafter planned first to seize the San Juan Heights. Though the hills were well defended by 750 Spanish soldiers in heavily for-tified positions, the Americans, by taking and holding them, would have a commanding view and a tactical advantage over the ten thousand–strong enemy in the city below. First, however, General Lawton's infantry was ordered to take the town of El Caney, four miles north of El Pozo Hill, to prevent a garrison of Spanish soldiers in that town from reinforcing those holding the San Juan Heights. Lawton was supported by a detach-ment of artillery commanded by Captain Allyn Capron, Sr., father of the Rough Riders' Captain Capron, who had been killed at Las Guasimas only a few days earlier. (The senior Capron later contracted typhoid fever and died in September 1898.)

Lawton estimated that the capture of El Caney would require about two hours, so the attack on the San Juan Heights was delayed until his troops held El Caney, at which time they would launch a coordinated charge on the heights. In the meantime, an artillery battery would begin firing from El Pozo Hill toward the San Juan Heights in an attempt to soften up enemy entrenchments. During this time, the Rough Riders and other units waited along the trail from El Pozo Hill until they received

orders to march toward the ford at the San Juan River, directly below the
San Juan Heights.[1]

After leaving camp [on June 30] we learned that our next
objective was El Pozo Hill. After marching for quite a while, we
saw a big house on the hill, tilting to the left of the trail. Captain Capron [Sr.] took his battery in that direction and set up
cannon for action. Here we [U.S. Army Signal Corps] had a
large balloon with two men in it. Big ropes tethered it down
and it rose about half a mile into the air so the observers could
see every move the Spanish made. The underbrush here was so
thick that a person could hardly get through. There was firing
here, but we were nearing the Spanish in their trenches. Farther
on, this road widened out to about 30 feet, and our army began
cutting the underbrush, getting ready to set up the bigger guns.

When everything was set, we could hear the artillery opening fire on the Spanish, but they never answered fire for about
thirty minutes. Finally, their artillery began shooting back. Our
troops had lined up to the left of the artillery on El Pozo Hill.
The order came to count down eight men on the line, and each
eighth man was to go [to the tilting house, a supply point on El
Pozo Hill, to] get boxes of shells for the rapid-fire guns. Each
trooper was ordered to carry an extra box of these shells in his
pack.

I was an eighth man, one of the boys assigned to retrieve the
shells. Just as I got around the house to pick up my eight boxes
of shells, an enemy artillery round burst in front of me, part of
it hitting my hand. I picked up the shells and started back. Just
then a shell hit the top of this house. The roof was tile and there
were several Cubans stationed on top of it. When the shell hit,
Cubans and tile were scattered all over the country.

When I had been detailed to go after shells, a man by the
name of Long was on one side of me, and a man named
Mitchell was on the other. After I had stepped out of line, a
shell burst where I had been standing and wounded both of

these men. If I had not been told to go after those shells, I most probably would not have been able to write this story today. When I got back, I saw Long lying there with his leg shot off below the knee. I found that the rest of the troop had moved around the hill to the east, and as I had left my gun at the line, there I was with plenty of shells but no gun. I told Long that I would help him down under the hill but he told me to go on as he thought he could crawl to safety on his own.

I pulled out then looking for my troop and found them two hundred yards on down the road. They were headed toward San Juan Hill and Santiago. The hill was covered in trenches and was held by the Spanish Army. We were almost under our big balloon, and the men above kept hollering down about the location of the enemy in their trenches. One of the men in the balloon was shot. The captain hollered up and asked the man if he wanted to come down but he said that he didn't. The balloon was brought down in a short time anyway.

When we reached the San Juan River, we called to halt. We had come through a ten-wire entanglement, and were forced to bunch up to get the barbed wire down. During this time we were under heavy fire. The Tenth Cavalry Regiment, known as Buffalo Soldiers, was to our left and near us. Orders came for us to deploy to the right, and that took us across the river into a glade of high grass in sight of the enemy trenches. We were ordered to take cover and wait.

The fire from the enemy had intensified, and as we took cover, I could hear the bullets whizzing through the grass as if they were mowing it down in front of us, but when I looked up I didn't find any grass missing, but some of the boys were.

While pinned down by deadly Spanish rifle fire, the Rough Riders suffered what Roosevelt called "the most serious loss that I and the regiment could have suffered." Captain William Owen "Buckey" O'Neill of Arizona, former newspaperman, mayor of Prescott, and Grand Canyon explorer, died instantly when hit in the head by a Mauser bullet. O'Neill

and some other officers subscribed to the theory that they should never take
cover. Rather, they purposely exposed themselves simply for the effect on
their men. It was ten in the morning when O'Neill strolled around in front
of his troopers, offering them encouragement. While O'Neill was pacing
and chatting, Spanish rifle bullets came "whizzing through the grass," one
of them fatally striking him.

All morning long, casualties mounted among the fifteen American reg-
iments tasked to take the heights. By midday, it became apparent that
General Lawton's troops were engaged in heavy fighting at El Caney and
would be unable to join in the attack. Roosevelt and other officers pleaded
with their superiors for a chance to move forward rather than die hunkered
down in the grass. Correspondent Richard Harding Davis later reported
that the troopers could not move back because the trails behind them were
wedged full of men, and they were being "shot to pieces" where they hud-
dled in the grass and tree line. Assaulting the hill was the only option.[2]

Now it was at this point that Colonel Roosevelt overstepped
his orders and gave his own command to charge the hill. Away
he went in the lead, riding his fine bay horse named "Little
Texas," waving his hat and heading for the enemy trenches.
There were eight men right behind him, riding as close as possible. They hit a ten-wire entanglement and tore it down, crossing to the enemy side in short time. Cuban troops followed
behind, and to the left was General Wheeler with his colored
troops, and on the right was General Sumner with his troops.
First we took the trenches by the blockhouse and the Spanish
retreated on up the San Juan Hill. No one stopped on Kettle
Hill because there were no trenches there, so our troops fell
into the trenches at San Juan Hill.

During the charge, I remember something that happened to
two old pals. One was Marcellus "Sel" Newcomb from Kingfisher, Oklahoma, and the other, Tom Holmes from Newkirk,
Oklahoma. They were both shot in this charge, but Tom was
hit first. Tom was rather high-tempered and when he was shot
in the knee, he thought that Sel Newcomb had hit him in the

knee with a rock. He stopped and asked him why in thunder had he hit him with a rock, but he fell shortly and Sel Newcomb got hit [wounded], too. It seems odd to me that in this action I would remember some of these things, but under fire of this kind, it is often those things that we remember best.

Two hilltops, separated by a ravine, dominated the San Juan Heights. Both were fortified with blockhouses. The northernmost of these was known as Kettle Hill, so named by the soldiers because of two huge iron kettles located at an abandoned sugar mill. Kettle was the first hill taken that day when Roosevelt acted not on his own, as McGinty and some others had thought, but on orders from General Sumner to move forward. Roosevelt broke from the tree line along the river astride his horse "Little Texas," with his men behind him. He rode quickly toward the Ninth Cavalry, which held the position to his front. When he called out, "If you don't wish to go forward, let my men pass," the response was spontaneous. The American forces surged forward and up the hill. Roosevelt, the only man on horseback, soon was in the lead of the swarm of dismounted cavalry and infantrymen as they charged to drive the Spaniards from their stronghold.

Upon reaching their objective, there was no respite. In the words of McGinty, "No one stopped on Kettle Hill." Through his field glass, Roosevelt could see American forces assaulting nearby San Juan Hill. He noted that "the proper thing to do was to help them out."

The move up San Juan Hill had begun about the same time the Rough Riders charged Kettle Hill. First Lieutenant Jules Ord of the Sixth Infantry wanted to move forward and asked General Hamilton Hawkins, who commanded the First Brigade, for permission to do so. Hawkins refused at first, but Ord, in an unusual exchange between a commanding general and a staff officer, begged to lead a charge.

"If you do not FORBID it, I will start it," Ord implored. "I only ask you not to refuse permission. We cannot stay here." Finally, without giving permission or refusing it, Hawkins said, "God bless you and good luck!" Ord smiled and with a pistol in one hand and a saber in the other, shouted, "Come on—come on, you fellows! Come on—we can't stop here."

As American Gatling guns raked Spanish positions on San Juan Hill, Roosevelt led the Rough Riders down the slopes of Kettle Hill and up San Juan in support of the advancing infantry. The Spaniards fought furiously but finally retreated. Once on the summit, Roosevelt found himself the ranking American officer with orders to hold his position "at all hazards" and advance no farther.

The hectic battle lasted about two hours before the Spanish flag was finally pulled down. Among Rough Rider casualties was seventeen-year-old Roy V. Cashion of Hennessey, Oklahoma Territory, one of the first Oklahomans to die on foreign soil in service to his country. The recent graduate of Hennessey High School had chosen the subject "Cuba Libre" for his senior oration. In 1900, the small town of Cashion, in southeastern Kingfisher County, Oklahoma, was named in his honor.[3]

We could see the city [of Santiago] from the hill. Many Spaniards had been left dead in the trenches; most of them had been shot in the head. When we reached these trenches we stopped, as it was late and quite a number of men were missing. We could not figure out what happened to them until the next morning. About sixty of our men had charged on over the hill, ending up where the Spanish could still fire at them from their trenches.

During the night the Spaniards had made several unsuccessful counterattacks on our men who were in these forward trenches, resulting in close combat. The enemy then dug in just across a small draw from them. At daylight our men tried using knives to dig trenches back toward us. When we discovered their location that morning, we had no way of helping them get back to us until nightfall again.

According to Roosevelt, these men were not necessarily trapped, but in the forward firing line trenches, which had been hastily dug at night on unfamiliar ground. As such, the trenches had no covered approaches that allowed the men to move to the rear area without exposure to enemy fire. The main body of Roosevelt's troops remained beyond the crest of the hill

The monument in Hennessey, Oklahoma, to seventeen-year-old hometown boy Roy Cashion, the first Oklahoma Territory Rough Rider to die in Cuba. Authors' Collection.

and out of view, and every six hours he relieved those in the forward trenches by what he called an "exciting" method. He waited until there was a lull in the enemy firing, then sent a relief party running over the hill and down toward the forward trenches. The new men then "tumbled into the trenches every which way."

After that, Roosevelt said, "the men who had been relieved got out as best they could," one at a time, and ran back to safety on the protected side of the hill. Each time the exchange was made it resulted in a tremendous outburst of firing from the Spanish lines, but the "firing proved quite harmless."

This action on July 2 amounted to a standoff, but the prospects of waiting out the Spanish in a siege were dismal because the jungle climate took an exacting toll on American forces. Afternoon downpours left their

*trenches a mosquito breeding ground, and dysentery, malaria, and yellow
fever spread rapidly through the American ranks.*[4]

July 2 turned out terribly hot and Colonel Roosevelt knew
that the boys [in the forward trenches] could not stay there all
day without food or water. The morning was sultry with a slight
fog, and when the sun came out, it bore down with intensity.

Colonel Roosevelt and Captain Kane decided to send some
tomatoes, hardtack, and coffee to the boys [in the forward
trenches]. I was standing close by when the officers were talking about trying to get food to them. When they asked for volunteers, I stepped up and told them I would try it. When I
started to go, Colonel Roosevelt said, "Wait, I'll go with you."

Captain Kane replied, "No, Colonel Roosevelt, if anyone
goes with him, I will go. The whole regiment is depending on
you, but no one is depending on either of us."

Then I told Captain Kane and the colonel that there was no
sense risking two men, so I took a case of food on my shoulders
and was humped over trying to stay as close to the ground as I
could. The firing seemed to come in a bit of crossfire. A couple
of bullets hit the case of food, and tomato juice began running
down on my face and back, but I never was hit myself. When I
reached the boys, I stayed there and dug out a hole to crawl into.

A short time later, another of our boys, Dick Shanafelt, made
it over with a big can of coffee, and as luck would have it, he
never got a scratch.

*Regimental officers obviously felt there was more to McGinty's feat
than his brief description here. He received a distinguished service citation
for "Carrying food to trenches under heavy fire."*

*Thirty-eight-year-old New York City bachelor Woodbury Kane was
another of the "Fifth Avenue Boys." A friend of Roosevelt, Kane was a
polo player, horseman, foxhunter, and yachtsman who wound up forming
one of the most unlikely friendships in the regiment by becoming close pals
with Billy McGinty.*

Nineteen-year-old Dick Shanafelt, originally from Lawrence, Kansas, but more recently from Perry, Oklahoma, was in Troop D. He later contracted yellow fever, and after a year of convalescing, volunteered to serve in the Philippines. When he completed his military service, Shanafelt worked for twenty-eight years with the Bureau of Indian Affairs in Muskogee, Oklahoma. He was one of only four surviving Rough Riders when he died in 1967.[5]

To avoid being shelled by the Spanish artillery, the boys started digging a trench back toward our position. They would dig in the ground just deep enough to hide their bodies and keep inching forward as they completed more trenches. Some of the main regiment [on the hill] tunneled toward us until we finally reached the main trenches of San Juan Hill.

There was high grass and underbrush scattered everywhere around the base of the hills, and when a man went down or was killed, he was hard to find. There seemed to be hundreds of buzzards down there. They followed us all around the battlefield. When someone died, it was only a short time until the buzzards were working on him. Often, this was the only way we had of finding the dead, and the burial detail usually just buried them on top of the ground by heaping shovels of dirt over them. This was repeated many, many times.

There was a regular burying squad that followed us in the field, and after this charge of the hills, they had a big job because there were thousands of Spanish killed, and sixteen hundred of our men, dead and wounded.

I do not wish to judge too harshly, but burying the dead was one aspect of the army that wasn't taken care of as well as it might have been. Of course, as General Sherman had remarked before, "War is Hell;" a conclusion that the burial detail seemed to have reached. Unfortunately, many of our wounded might have been saved if they had been reached in time, but there wasn't much chance for a man living long when badly wounded and losing blood, lying there under the hot, blazing July sun.

Roosevelt recorded American losses at San Juan as 1,071 killed and wounded. The number for the Spanish Army varies from 1,200 to 1,700, in addition to another 2,000 enemy soldiers found to be sick or wounded in Santiago hospitals when that city fell.

The Stillwater Gazette of July 21, 1898, reported that McGinty had written a letter to a local man expressing, "a sincere desire that the war with Spain be brought to a close as soon as possible." According to the Gazette, McGinty "had been at the front long enough to satisfy his curiosity and convince him that the saying 'war is hell' is true. He says that their chief trouble down there now is getting food. It has been raining almost every day since the army landed and the roads over which provision trains must pass are in horrible condition, twelve miles a day with a four mule team being a good day's travel."[6]

The Siege of Santiago lasted from about July 3 to July 17. At the blockhouse on San Juan Hill we had two rapid-fire guns. The Stevens boys, nationally know as gunsmiths, had donated them to the Rough Riders. The guns had no cooling system and after firing for a time, they would be red hot, and the boys would have to let them cool for a bit.

A man named Parker had a dynamite gun. He was stationed along our line and would shoot over our heads. It didn't make much noise when going over; just a wind-like whistling noise and it looked like a blue streak going through the air.

The "rapid-fire" guns were automatic Colt guns on tripods. They replaced the artillery pieces that had been moved off the hill the night of July 1. The rapid-fire guns were too heavy for troops to carry, and were moved about only when packmules could be found. Some confusion exists as to who donated these nonmilitary-issue guns. All sources agree on Woodbury Kane and Joseph Sampson Stevens, but others include William Tiffany, Jr. Roosevelt lists the donors as Kane, Stevens, Tiffany, and "one or two other of the New York men." Stevens, of royal French descent, may have been a gunsmith, but was not related to the Stevens Firearms Company.

The Sims-Dudley "dynamite gun" did not actually fire dynamite. The experimental, breech-loading artillery piece normally used compressed air

Teddy Roosevelt and his Rough Riders at the crest of San Juan Hill, July 1, 1898. Courtesy of the Library of Congress, Washington D.C.

to launch a projectile containing nitro-based gelatin. In Cuba, this field gun could not carry a compressor, so it used a small powder charge to compress the air needed to fire the projectile, which was fitted with either a time or a percussion fuse. When fired like a mortar from behind the hill, it did not betray its location. Lieutenant John Henry Parker, a West Point career army man, commanded the Fifth Corps' Gatling gun detachment, which included the dynamite gun and the rapid-fire Colts.[7]

The officer would stand up with Teddy Roosevelt and look though field glasses to locate some of the enemy guns that were doing the most damage. Then they trained the dynamite gun on the location. They found one such enemy gun under a big mango tree. It had a Red Cross emblem over it, and knowing that our army wouldn't fire on a red cross, the enemy used this as a shield from our gunfire.

Parker trained his dynamite gun on the spot, and just as he went to fire it, the firing pin failed to set it off. A cap of some kind was used to detonate the charge and fire it. A man who worked with Parker on this big gun had a hammer, so he picked it up and hit the cap with the hammer. Away went that dynamite and hit a bull's eye, and up in the air went the mango tree and part of the crew and their gun. The enemy gun had been set in cement, and could only be turned part of the way around, facing our troops. It would have been useless to the Spanish if we had come up on the side of it. From then on, the officers watched for the Red Cross emblems to see if the enemy was using them as gun traps. I believe our dynamite gun was a great help in winning this war, for the Spanish couldn't figure out what kind of a shell was doing so much damage.

Before the start of the Siege of Santiago, our army called a conference with the Spanish, and both armies raised white flags. Eight officers of the Spanish Army met eight officers of our army close to the blockhouse on San Juan Hill. Our officers gave orders for the Spanish to surrender or stand siege, and gave them twenty-four hours to get the women and children out of Santiago. The Spanish wanted more than twenty-four hours to give them time to communicate with Spain.

The "conference with the Spanish" McGinty refers to came on the morning of July 3, when General Shafter sent a dispatch to the enemy demanding they surrender or his forces would shell the city of Santiago. The Spanish ultimately rejected the offer.

At midmorning, the Spanish fleet, tucked safely away in Santiago Harbor since the invasion began, steamed toward the open sea and the waiting blockade of Admiral Sampson's fleet. In a fierce, four-hour sea fight, every Spanish ship was sunk, disabled, or beached in flames. The Americans suffered slight damage to one ship with one sailor killed.[8]

Now this was the first time that I had seen General Shafter on the front line. He had a bodyguard of about six men with him. He was exceptionally big and fat, nearly covering his horse. I don't know how much he weighed but he was plenty big. Even so, he seemed to handle his horse mighty well in spite of all his bulk.

When the twenty-four hours were up, our army took down the truce flag, but the enemy kept theirs up for about thirty minutes longer. Then the firing began again. They ceased firing at sundown, but about nine o'clock at night they started up on us again.

At first most of the officers were out of their trenches. We were under a heavy fire, but well entrenched and not in much danger. From our trenches it seemed as though the enemy rifle fire was like prairie fire in the distance. We would rise up and empty our rifles at that blaze of prairie fire, and then get down and load them. Our rifles held seven [*sic*] shells. We kept this up for some time.

General Leonard Wood was instrumental in obtaining the Krag-Jorgensen carbine for the Rough Riders, the first army-issue weapon to use the relatively new smokeless powder, which did not leave a puff of smoke betraying the shooter's location. This bolt-action, 30-caliber rifle held five rounds in the magazine and one in the chamber compared with the army's older 45–70, single-shot Springfield Trapdoor rifles that used black powder and emitted a cloud of white smoke. The Krag's shells could also be used in the Gatling gun, and their lighter weight allowed soldiers to carry more ammunition. The entire Spanish Army used smokeless powder, but two American infantry units and all of its artillery units still used black powder, making their positions easy to spot. As Roosevelt lamented, "Our artillery made one or two efforts to come into action on the firing-line of the infantry [during the fight for San Juan Hill], but the black powder rendered each attempt futile."[9]

After we had been firing for some time, I had just got up to empty my rifle at the enemy when Teddy Roosevelt came down our line on top of the trenches. There was heavy firing from the enemy and I didn't see how he kept from getting hit. He hollered out an order to cease firing, but I had already started to fire my rifle, so I went ahead and emptied my gun. Roosevelt was coming close to where I was then, and as I jumped back into the trench, he hollered down and wanted to know "who did that."

I just hunkered down in the trench and never said a word. He asked two or three times who it was, and I thought he was going to jump right down into the trench, and if he had, I would have had to beat the dickens for he certainly was mad. This is about the maddest I ever saw him, and I don't know why I ever did that, for it certainly was the wrong thing to do.

The next morning, I found out why he had given the order to cease firing. Colonel Roosevelt had figured that the Spanish were trying this night attack to get a bearing on the exact location of our lines and our firing at night made it easy for them to locate us, just as in the daytime when the army used black powder.

After firing those shots, I sure was sorry because Colonel Roosevelt was good to me and to all the boys for that matter. If you were around him much, it was a cinch that you would like him. He was kind and considerate under all kinds of conditions. He had a way about him that would make a tramp or a millionaire feel at home in his presence.

I noticed him several times when he went by the boys. When they rose to salute he would motion them to sit still and say, "No need to salute me on the battlefield, take care of yourself and rest. Saluting is all right in its place, but here we are all equal." He meant it, too, for he was speaking for himself and all the boys. Some of the officers in the regulars thought that you should salute them anyway, no matter where you were.

I remember one fellow that was by my side in the trenches. His name was Jakie Allen [*sic*]. We were in a trench taken from the Spanish, and he would go along where the dead Spanish lay, and go through their pockets to see what he could find. He would cut the buttons and badges off the dead Spanish officers, and when I asked him what he was doing, he told me he was getting souvenirs to take home. I told him that if he didn't stop taking chances around those dead Spaniards, he would get shot and wouldn't need any souvenirs. He was always looking to see what he could find.

On about July 6, the Spanish started a fierce bombardment. We were on the San Juan Hill that circled the town and the bay. We were about four miles from the mouth of the bay and there was shooting going on down there. We never learned about it until later, but it was at this time a sailor by the name of Hobson, with eight other men, tried to block the harbor by running an American ship up in the narrow straits and sinking it. The men got the ship turned about three-quarters of the way around and sank it, but did not succeed in blocking the harbor. The sailors swam ashore on the Morro Castle side of the bay and were taken prisoners. I believe they were taken on in to Santiago.

It was a few days after this that the Spanish raised their flag, and we raised ours to see what they wanted. They were asking more time to get the women and children out of Santiago, and also to hear from Spain. They, too, wanted to trade prisoners, and they brought them up to our line. We traded them two for one. Hobson was one of the men brought up, and the prisoners were all dressed in white. That was the only time I ever saw Hobson.

Actually, it was on June 3, while the Rough Riders were still in Tampa, that Navy Lieutenant Richmond P. Hobson and seven American sailors steered the doomed collier Merrimac *into the channel of Santiago Harbor in an effort to block it. During this attempt, a shell severed her steering mechanism, causing her to sink before reaching the point where the ship was to be scuttled. The Spanish took the daring sailors prisoner, and on July 6, the day McGinty refers to here, they were returned to the American lines in a prisoner exchange, resulting in gunfire and cheering as part of the celebration.*[10]

Our officers and the Spanish met about fifty yards from the blockhouse. After the dickering was over and our prisoners were back, Hobson told us about his experience in the bay. All I can remember was his saying that the Spanish had treated him fairly well, but we did not get quite as good a report about treatment from some of the other prisoners.

The truce flag stayed up about two days this time and everything was mighty quiet all around. About eight or ten others and I went over to the Spanish side of the trenches where there was a well and some San Juan Hill trees for shade. Some of the boys laid down in the shade and wrote letters back home. They told us that these letters would need no stamps, as all we had to do was write on them, "Soldier's Letters."

I had promised to write a letter to Robert Lowry when I got there, so I laid down in the shade and started writing. I had been there for quite awhile trying to think of something to write and not paying much attention to the other boys or the truce flags. I could see our flag, and all at once the firing started. I looked and our flag was down, and looked over to where the other boys were and they were gone, too. I jumped up and made a run for the trenches, and as I jumped, someone hollered "What do you mean?" I cut him short by saying "Fellow, I mean to get into these trenches."

After the firing started, we were deployed around to the right. This was to the north of a wide road about one hundred feet across that led out of Santiago to the east toward the small town of El Caney. This town was laid out like our towns back home, built around a square.

We were camped upon the hill, which was about a mile from the San Juan River where we got our water. The river was a nice mountain stream, banked with big mango trees and heavy underbrush that formed quite a jungle. Now it was a big job to carry water from this point, and we were about worn out. We were supposed to boil all the water, but sometimes in our hurry we didn't always do that. We were camped there during the time the truce flag was raised up and back down at intervals. Sometimes the Spanish would lower their flag and start shelling us, and then we would lower ours and return fire.

At that time, the women, children and old men were evacuating Santiago and heading for El Caney. This was a pitiful sight and one I shall never forget. Both old women and young women, babes in arms, barefoot children, old men and the feeble would go along that road, loaded down with all the worldly possessions that they could carry. Some had bundles that were even too big for pack mules. The road was hot and gravelly, and the rich and poor alike traveled together. Most of their bundles were made from big sheets that they laid down, put their belongings in the middle of, then gathered up the four corners, carrying it on their backs. Some loads were so heavy that they would carry them only a short distance, then set them down and rest. A few people had some sort of vehicle but most were afoot. They kept glancing back and all of them had a look of fear and horror on their faces. They were afraid the firing would start any minute and they would be caught in the shelling.

That sight of women and children is still etched in my mind, and I can see those poor creatures, many so thin and skinny that they looked as if they had not eaten for weeks. They would stop the soldiers and beg for a few bits of food. Some of them looked so weak that I couldn't see how they were strong enough to navigate.

Our boys were in almost as bad a shape. We had only a small amount of food, and many of the boys shared what little they had with some of the stragglers. It was one continuous mass of people streaming along this road as Santiago was evacuated. They all sat down and rested together, for this was one place where rank never took any stock of hunger, thirst, and weariness.

We had plenty of hardtack onboard ship down at the sea, but no way of getting it to us. Here is where I offered Ed Norris, of Pawnee, a five-dollar gold piece for a can of what we called horsemeat. The boys only had a few cans and it would have taken big money to have bought it. The toughest, hardest poker game I ever saw in my life was played here. The stakes were a few cans of horsemeat, and some of the hardtack we had from the boat. The hardtack had been left on the lower decks of the boat, so it was molded, but we cut the mold off the sides and ate it anyway.

I was on water detail one day and went down to the river about a mile away. The boys were not allowed to wash or bathe in this stream for it was our sole means of drinking water. One way the boys did get by with using this stream for washing, was to go down near the river, dig a hole in the sand and line it with their rain coat, then by filling this with water, it made a good washing tub.

I had picked up a pack mule that had been shot in the shoulder. He was lame, but got well in a short time. I thought I might get a packsaddle some place, so I went to the pack train to look for one that had been thrown away and it was there I ran across an old friend. His name was "Black" Stanley. His first name came from his noticeably dark complexion. He was chief packer and he treated me real nice, introducing me to all the boys and showing me around. He told me that I was the only one he had seen over there that he knew. He even tried to get me to join up with his outfit. I told him that I was satisfied where I was, but we did have one man transferred to his outfit, a chap by the name of Wright.

All of "Black" Stanley's kind treatment in Cuba reminded me of a different kind of treatment I got when I first met him. The first time I saw "Black" Stanley was in the fall of 1892, when one day I rode up to his chuck wagon. He was just west of the government beef pasture near Ft. Supply [western Oklahoma]. I had been out looking for some horses that the wrangler let get away and stopped to see if he had seen them. He asked me to stay the night as it was then evening. While I was there he plied me with question after question, as if I was a horse thief or outlaw. After breakfast next morning, as I rode out of camp, I thought, "I would have rather laid out in the high grass all night with the coyotes, as bed mate with you another night."

But in Cuba, it was different. When you met someone you knew, the past was forgotten and it seemed like a binding link to some lost chord that longed for home and friends you knew. "Black" Stanley helped me get a packsaddle. I guess he thought I had some old Spanish mule, for I was a good scrounger, especially when it came to transportation because I never liked to walk much.

I was perplexed for a time as what to use to haul water in but finally worked it out. I just took two of those big bamboo poles and removed the pith from them. Then I tied them with the butt up to each side of the packsaddle so that they fitted right up against the mule's shoulders. When I went down to the river to fill these bamboo buckets, which held about four buckets full of water, I tied my pony to the limb of a mango tree, and led the pack mule into the river.

I had blindfolds on the mule for he was afraid of the bamboo poles and every time he saw them hanging on his side he would do everything within his power to try to get away. This time when I went to dip up the water, the mule flopped his head and the blindfold slipped down. Then he struck at me, knocking me over into the water and taking off toward the opposite side of the river. There was thick underbrush forming a heavy jungle on that side, and the mule didn't get far until he got hung up in it.

I got up just about the time he struck the edge of the jungle and I happened to see another movement close by. It was a man in a Spanish uniform. On up the river a ways, a fellow from our troop by the name of Cockney Carroll was washing some clothes in the sand. He saw my mule get hung up in the heavy underbrush, so he came to help me get him loose. I grabbed my rifle on the bank, slipped down into the river, and crossed over.

A person couldn't see any distance in that heavy underbrush if he stood up, but if he laid down and crawled, he could see about sixty feet ahead. I crawled along and saw that Spaniard up ahead, sitting with his rifle between his knees and watching my mule. I slipped up to about thirty feet of him and stopped. I had my rifle out in front of me as I crawled along, and when I stopped I threw my gun on him, and then happened to think I didn't have a cartridge into the barrel. I gave it [the bolt] a quick jerk throwing in a load. About that time the Spaniard heard the click of the lock and just as he turned, I hollered for him to throw down his gun and stick 'em up.

Cockney Carroll reached my mule about that time and he took the Spaniard's gun and found that it wasn't even loaded. He was out of ammunition and had probably gotten cut off from his troops and was hiding, waiting for night to try to slip through our lines. He had probably been a sharpshooter with the Spanish Army. Carroll took him back to camp [as a prisoner], and I untangled my pack mule, got his blinders back on, and took a load of water back to camp. I used this method for packing water, and we always had plenty of it.

CHAPTER 3

Surrender, Occupation, and Homeward Bound

IT wasn't long after that when word came from Spain for their army to surrender. Our regiment did not have much duty at the surrender, but the Spaniards all marched down and put their guns in a big pile, and I mean there was a big pile of guns when it was finished.

The formal Spanish surrender finally came on July 17, thus ending the Siege of Santiago and a miserable two weeks in the trenches for the Rough Riders and other troops.[1]

After that, we received orders to move on up the mountain and we made camp along a nice little stream. General Joe Wheeler was camped just above us with his colored troops and while in camp he was visited by his daughter [Annie] several times. She must have been with the hospital corps. She came up from headquarters and walked right through our camp. She was a tall girl, then being around twenty-three years old, I judge.

We had a lot of sickness and fever among the soldiers and it was there when Lieutenant Tiffany broke down with some very serious and contagious disease. I had been taking his food up to him on a hill where they had moved him for isolation. One morning I started out with his food from the officers' mess tent, and I was stopped by a sentry and given orders not to go on up. I thought at first he was dead, but they found he had yellow fever and he did die a few days later, as did many others from some sort of jungle fever.

I was sure sorry to hear of Lieutenant Tiffany's passing, for he was a mighty swell fellow. He seemed to like me and he, being in charge of the rapid-fire guns, had one day asked me to try shooting them. I wasn't too anxious to do it, but finally did, and the gun went off four times before I could take my finger off the trigger. He was the son of the New York jeweler, Tiffany.

William Tiffany, Jr., the popular New Yorker, died of yellow fever in late July after his evacuation to Boston on a hospital ship carrying many other sick troopers.[2]

We were camped along a small stream where we got our drinking water. Below it was a nice water hole, and we were allowed to swim there. A sergeant of our troop named Sherman Bell was swimming one day and [his hernia] was badly ruptured when he slipped and fell. Four of the doctors there tried to help him but could do him no good.

Sherman Bell, a former deputy marshal from Cripple Creek, Colorado, was so "tough," according to Roosevelt, that they accepted him as a Rough Rider knowing he already had a serious hernia condition. Bell limped through the jungles and across the hills most of the time, but always seemed to stay up with the troops despite the pain. The afternoon before the battle of San Juan Hill, he was ordered to a field hospital to wait for an ambulance to take him to the rear and eventual transport back to the United States. After dark, some fellow troopers helped him sneak off into hiding so the ambulance would leave without him. Roosevelt found him on the line with his troop the next morning. Bell told his Colonel he would "rather die fighting" if he must, and Roosevelt said he didn't have the "heart to send him back."

Bell performed "splendid service" that day and during their time in the trenches, but his condition worsened again after the fall in the stream.[3]

They finally decided that to ease him he should be taken at once to the headquarters' general hospital. His condition had grown very serious and they immediately detailed me and one of Bell's friends named Ben Daniels, to take him down the mountain. The only transportation was a one-horse cart. They told me that those types of carts lasted for a long time because they could hardly be worn out.

I got the outfit together and ready to go, and they shot him full of morphine and told us we had better get him to the hospital before the drug played out. We put Sherman Bell in this two-wheel cart. The back band of the harness was padded like a saddle, and it fitted right on the back of the mule with the weight mostly on the mule's back. When we first started, Ben Daniels walked behind while I sat up in the back of the cart with the rifle in my hands. We had to go through a very spooky part of the jungle, although I don't think there was much danger of anything.

The walking was mighty hard, and it was hot, too, and in a short time, Ben was just rolling in sweat. I kept telling him we would have to hurry, but he would get behind, and I would have to pull up and wait. He kept telling me that there wasn't room for both of us in the cart, but I told them that if he didn't get in I wasn't going to stop for him again. Ben Daniels held a higher rank than I did and I should not have talked like that to him but I guess he figured he was the same as I since we fussed back and forth all the time.

The road down the mountain pass to the hospital was rough. I kept whipping the mule trying to hurry, and Ben kept telling me that I would kill Sherman Bell if I didn't slow up, but I knew that if we didn't get there before the morphine played out, we would have lots of trouble.

I didn't pay much attention to Ben's hollering, for he was having a time holding on to the cart, and couldn't do much anyway. That old cart hadn't been greased for many a month and the wheels would squall real loud every time they turned around. There we were going down the mountainside "lickety-split," the wheels squalling and Ben Daniels trying to hold on, yelling above the noise for me to "take it easy."

Benjamin Franklin Daniels was described as "a very large, hawk-eyed man," who had once been a Kansas lawman. Roosevelt said, "He viewed the dangers of battle with philosophic calm. Such a man was, in reality, a veteran even in his first fight, and was a tower of strength to the recruits in his part of the line."[4]

Sherman Bell's head was about a foot or more below his feet the way we had laid him in the cart, and the morphine had relaxed his body so that he took each bump with the cart. This, of course, was much better than if he had not relaxed because then he would have received more jarring around. We reached the hospital before the drug played out, and I gave a note from our doctors to the head doctor there, and Ben and I took it easier back to camp.

When we returned, the doctors were anxious to know how we made out. I told Dr. [Harry] Thorpe how Ben had griped about jarring Sherman Bell too much, and he told me that he didn't think it made any difference, as he didn't hold much chance for him anyway. I never thought much more about it, just figuring that I would never see Sherman Bell alive again.

After the war, when I was in New York City, I became ill and was hospitalized there. One day a man and his girlfriend came to visit me, and who should he be but Sherman Bell. He introduced me to the lady by saying, "Here is the McGinty that saved my life in Cuba," and he gave her a line of bull about him and me.

I had thought him to be a truthful fellow, and must have looked at him like it was a mystery to me, for he said, "You act like you don't know what I'm talking about."

"Remember when I was in that awful fix in the mountains of Cuba?"

I told him, "Of course I remember that."

"Well," Sherman Bell went on, "The doctors told me that the trip down the mountainside was what saved my life. My head being lower than my feet, and because I was relaxed the jolts along the rough mountain side worked that rupture slowly back in and when I reached the hospital, the doctors did not need to operate, or do much, and I was already on the road to recovery."

While in camp on that hill in Cuba, Lieutenant [James Robert] Church became very ill, and couldn't eat anything. The doctors figured out if they had a wild guinea fowl, they could make some broth out of it, and they might be able to get him to eat that. They detailed Ben Daniels and me to get a guinea. There were quite a number of them, but shooting one was a big job. I never saw one on the ground and they fly fast and high, faster than a quail or dove. They had been hunted so much they were plenty wild.

Lieutenant "Rob" Church served as regimental surgeon. Son of the U.S. Senate's librarian and former Princeton football player, he was a hero to all Rough Riders for the way he conscientiously tended the wounded. He often trudged back and forth along the trails, soaked with blood and sweat, carrying the wounded from the battlefield to his makeshift tent hospital. Following the war, Church was awarded the Medal of Honor for repeatedly being "subjected to heavy fire and great exposure and danger."[5]

If we had a shotgun it would have been easier, but Ben never said anything, just picked up a rifle, and I grabbed mine, and we started out. After we had started, I told Ben that this looked like a big job to me, but he said that we would find the guineas and it would work out. We hadn't gone far when we scared up two or three. I jerked my gun to my shoulder to shoot, but Ben killed two before I could fire. I had always thought I was a good rifle shot, but when I saw Ben shoot, I knew I was a back number. Ben was a sergeant, and a real soldier, and as near a perfect marksman as I ever saw. He had been a peace officer in Kansas.

I found out that many of the Rough Riders were excellent marksmen. They would throw up empty cans and fill them full of holes with their six-shooters before they could hit the ground. They not only could shoot but were also excellent horsemen. They were brave, daring, and adventurous, and withstood many hardships in Cuba where our ranks were taken in fever and sickness, as well as death. To those who died in Cuba, whether by bullets or by sickness, I would gladly pay tribute for there never was a finer, braver bunch of men; all of them were tried and true.

After the surrender, some of the officers came up the line and gave us orders not to go over to El Caney, the little town to the east of us. It was only a short distance over in the foothills of that range of mountains that circled Santiago. I never thought much of going over there, but they didn't tell us why they didn't want us to go.

The day after these orders came I asked a trooper named Weitzel about it. He was around headquarters a lot and had been doing orderly work. He didn't seem to care for much of anything but a good time and liked to see everything that was going on. He asked me, "Wonder what's the matter that we can't go over to El Caney?"

Eighteen-year-old John Frank Weitzel of Newkirk, Oklahoma Territory, was a member of Oklahoma National Guard's Company I when he and several other local guardsmen joined the Rough Riders' Troop D at Guthrie.[6]

He told me that he sure would like to see the place. We both knew that if we went, it would have to be at night, and he said that he thought we could find the way after dark. He didn't have a horse, so he proposed that I get one for him. I told him that I thought we could work it out, so we waited until that night and went out west of our camp where some horses were picketed. I figured if anything happened we could jump off the horses and run and no one would know who we were. We got the horses all right. One belonged to a man named Addison

Hall, and the other to General Joe Wheeler. We led them away from where they were picketed and when we thought we were safe we climbed on.

There was a small road through to El Caney with thick jungle timber on each side and we rode it on into town. El Caney had been a town of around eight hundred people with a square in the center. The town was now full of people of all nationalities and they were in every form of distress known to man, all sleeping and living here. It was one dirty hole if I ever saw one, and I think all they had to live on was mangos.

We rode through the square, which was all lit up. The people there were refugees from Santiago, and of many other places. Most were living in very small, unsanitary spaces and everyone looked skinny and sickly. I have seen that sort of filth among wild animals, but not humans. I believe that conditions there were the worst I had ever seen.

Weitzel and I rode on back to camp after a short stay in El Caney and staked the ponies at the same place we found them. I had a sort of homemade hammock in the trees not far from our row of dog tents, and had no trouble slipping into bed. The hammock was made of bamboo poles and rope, all tied together, and it made fairly good resting. I don't know how Weitzel got into his bed but he got away with it all right.

The next day Weitzel told me that he found out why we weren't supposed to go into town. He said that he heard that the refugees there had contracted yellow fever and the town was covered with the disease. We figured the best thing for us to do was to keep our trip under our hat, because if they found out, we would be sent to a quarantine pen for several days and that wasn't a very good place to be.

Maybe you think I wasn't scared for a while. I knew we might come down with yellow fever and we both felt bad about it. We should have been punished for such a trick. If we had known there was yellow fever there, we couldn't have been paid to go into town. I never could figure why that officer hadn't told us about the yellow fever, but as luck would have it, neither of us took down with a fever.

After the surrender, General Wood had been made governor-general over Cuba and was headquartered at Santiago. He asked Colonel Roosevelt to send his stuff over from the regimental headquarters, so the colonel asked me to get one of the boys and take it to him. This just suited me fine because I had a friend in G Troop that wanted to see the town real bad, and I did too.

I got a pack mule and loaded it up with General Wood's paraphernalia, then got my saddle horse and one for my friend Clarence Wright. After Colonel Roosevelt wrote out a pass for us, we were on our way and as happy as a pair of kids with new boots and brass toes on them. After going about a mile, we ran into a guard. He stopped us and asked for our pass. I fumbled around and finally dug into my pocket and found it, and after he looked it over, he told us that the pass was no good because it had to have General Shafter's name on it. It was four miles over to General Shafter's headquarters and we knew that by the time we made the rounds and went on into town, it would be so late we wouldn't have much time to look around.

Twenty-eight-year-old Clarence Wright of New Mexico's Troop G was from Springer, New Mexico, where he worked for the railroad before joining the Rough Riders.[7]

We rode off a short distance from the guard and talked it over, and we decided that Clarence was a better talker than I was, but I decided I would give him [the guard] a whirl. I went back but never got anywhere. I had turned to leave him when he called me back. He pointed over to the west and asked me if I saw those lone chimneys over there. I looked and saw some old ruins. He said that there was an old Spanish trench there and it went on into town. There was a big ten-wire fence there but no guard.

I told Clarence that we might try to get through some place, so we traveled up this fence line toward the old trench. There was brush on both sides of this fence and finally we reached a place where the fence went over a small knoll. I told Clarence that here was a good place to try to get through, so I tied my rope to one of the wires and pulled it loose. Then we tied it down to the bottom wire and got through. Maybe you think this was easy, but it was really quite a hard job.

After we got through the fence, we went into town by way of that old Spanish trench. There was a guard standing out in front of the Capitol [Governor's Palace] and I rode up to him and told him that we had General Wood's paraphernalia and that I wanted to take it in to him. He opened the door and said "ride in," so I did. I rode up to about twenty feet of where General Wood was sitting, and the first thing he said to me was, "Well, McGinty things are some different than in the states."

I said, "Yes, I could hardly ride my horse in and lead my pack mule into the capitol there."

As the military governor-general of Cuba, Wood had headquarters in the palace that once housed Spain's governor of Cuba, a rambling building located in Santiago's central plaza. Wood served in that capacity until 1902, and in 1904, then-president Roosevelt appointed him governor of Moro Province, the Philippines, and later as commander of the army's Philippine division. Wood declared himself a candidate for president in 1920 but lost the Republican nomination to Warren G. Harding.

Roosevelt was of the opinion that there was very little to do in the "dirty old Spanish city," although it was interesting to visit once or twice. Santiago's narrow streets were lined with little shops and its houses were of stained stucco, most having elaborate wrought iron trellises and carved balconies.[8]

I unpacked the mule and started back. General Wood never asked me to look around the Capitol and I was glad he didn't, for I was in a hurry to take a prowling trip around the city.

Clarence and I started out and went down the streets until we came to a saloon. We stopped and went in, and got several drinks of rum. We were feeling pretty good, so we went to an old theatre nearby but it was closed.

With nothing much to do we just rode around awhile, dropped into another joint or two for rum, then picked up a few things that Colonel Roosevelt wanted and packed them on our mule and started back to camp. We didn't go back by way of the trench and when we were leaving town, I saw a big dog crossing the street, so I roped him. I had quite a time getting him and finally told a Cuban who was standing nearby that he could turn him loose for me. We rode on down the road a spell, and there we ran into some guards. They were stopping folks and looking over their passes. I told Clarence that here was where we might have to go back to the trenches, but neither of us wanted to go that way. I told him we'd turn the pack mule loose, keep hitting him and drive him running on past the guards and ride by, not paying any attention to them. I told Clarence that if they started shooting at us to just keep on going because I didn't care, and I don't think Clarence did either. We had been shot at lots of times and it didn't matter if only one or two were shooting at us because I would rather be shot at than go back through those trenches.

The guards never even tried to stop us and after we had gone a short distance trying to stop our pack mule, the pack slipped and turned under the mule's belly and we lost a lot of things we had packed on. Clarence had bought a few bottles of rum to take back and he seemed more concerned about looking for them than anything. I didn't care about the rum because I had enough already. I finally roped the pack mule and we came back and picked up all the stuff that wasn't broken and started on for camp.

On down the road a piece, I saw a nice little bay horse. I told Clarence that it was a better pony than I was riding and if he would help me, I would catch him and make a trade. Since there was no one around to ask me for cash boot I went out and roped him and made the change.

I thought I had made a good trade but farther on down the road this pony began to limp, and the farther we went the lamer he got. Some one had turned him loose on account of his lameness, I guess. But we kept on going and came in sight of a big French mansion up on the side of the road. We went up to look it over and there were a lot of soldier boys there. It was a fine mansion and the boys were getting some lumber so they could make bunks.

I rode in at the front door and saw it was some fancy place. The inside floor was of marble, and there was a Cuban cooking coffee over a big fire built right on the marble floor. There were winding stairs going to the upper rooms, so I rode right by the Cuban, up the stairs and into all the rooms. Finally, I rode out on a huge balcony and could see our camp about a mile away. When I started down the stairs my horse refused to go but finally some of the boys gave him a push and down we went.

We went on into camp and gave Colonel Roosevelt the things he had sent for and turned in our pass. He asked us if the guards had accepted it, and we told him they would not. He then wanted to know how we got through. I told him we made it "OK," and he never said any more about it.

Before we left Cuba, Colonel Roosevelt asked me to pick him out a good saddle horse from some of the captured ponies. I tried several of them, but there was a little difference only in looks and not much in that. All those native horses were single-footed and they were nearly all small, just as our ponies were here about fifty years ago. I finally picked him out one, but I don't know what became of it.

A few days later I was resting in my hammock while we waited for orders to return to the good old United States and Clarence Wright, my friend from G Troop, came over and asked if I thought we could get a pass to go into Santiago at night to see the sights again. I told him that they were not issuing any night passes, but if he wanted to go to town it could be managed if we worked it right.

Clarence didn't believe it was possible since the camp was so well guarded. He had already tried to slip by one night on his own and got caught. He promised he would do about anything for me if he could get to go, so I told him to come back the next night and I would show him how to get by the guards. He still didn't believe we could do it, but said he would be back, figuring I had a pull with the guards and could get him through.

The next night Wright was over to my hammock raring to get going. After it got good and dark, we went out to a spot where I knew of some ponies that were staked out. I didn't know whose horses these were, only that they belonged to some of the officers. We kept our eyes on the guard that was up on a nearby ridge that ran to the north and south. We watched him and he would walk along the ridge to where he met another guard, and then they would both turn and go back as they each reached the limit of the guard post. I knew that the guards did not pay much attention to horses that were loose and wandering across the line grazing and feeding.

When the guard had gone to his south line, we crawled along in the high grass leading our horses, and slipped right through the line. After we had crawled past the line a ways and the guards had turned again, we got up and walked, leading the ponies until we were well out of sight. We then mounted and rode into town.

We were on a wide road that took us into the northeast part of the town. Shortly before we got there, we passed a big arena where they held all the bullfights. It was somewhat like the fairgrounds they build back home. As we reached town we began to wonder what we would do with our horses, and since the arena was lit up we rode inside. It was empty and we saw that the gate was made out of large timbers hung by huge hinges. I rode over behind this gate, and it was shaded pretty well from light, so we left the horses there. I tried to pull that big gate back more to hide them, but the hinges started squealing and I decided to let well enough alone.

We walked on into Santiago from there. The towns in Cuba are built quite different from most of ours in the states. There are few suburbs or outlying homes. They didn't build homes just here and there, they jammed them one right up against the other and built out as far as they wanted. Within about 150 feet from the bullfighting arena we were in the thick of town. Santiago was built in old-style architecture, and the buildings were flush with the street. The windows had iron bars crossing them, and many of the doors had sub doors made of iron.

We wandered around for a short while and finally went into a saloon. We sat down at a table to order drinks and a stranger came over and sat down with us. We asked his name but it has slipped my mind. He was not Spanish but had a dark complexion. He told us that at one time he had been a sailor. He seemed to be watching everybody and everything and, after a drink with us, he told Wright and me that it was bad business for us to be around there at night with our uniforms on. He said we would be lucky to even get out of the place and we should leave at once. We were the only Americans in there, and feelings about the war were naturally still high, so Wright and I talked it over and decided that maybe we should leave. We never had any trouble though, and slipped back into camp the way we left.

Wright always seemed to have plenty of money, and he liked action and used his money to get it too. He would have stayed in Santiago if I had just said the word. I was short on money most of the time and both of us, with a bit of adventure in our blood, made good pals.

One day [Captain] Woodbury Kane asked if there was any way that I could get hold of some extra horses. Most of the boys in camp were sick, and it was a two-mile trip to the railroad. The captain told me to take a man and try getting some horses after I told him I knew where some were. He didn't like

the system that I had figured out, but we agreed that most anything is fair in war. I picked a fellow named Edwin Emerson to
go with me. Many of you younger folks have read and studied
Emerson's books on history through your libraries and schools.
He was a great writer and was at one time war correspondent
in China. Emerson asked me why I had picked him, and I told
him that I just knew he would like to go, and since he was a
newspaperman and wanted to see everything in the war, he
could have first-hand information on how we transported the
sick soldiers.

*Edwin Emerson, Jr., a journalist from New York City, served as both
a war correspondent and a volunteer Rough Rider in Troop K. Graduated
from Harvard in 1891, he wrote on many subjects, ranging from the
Gutenberg Bible to a history of the nineteenth century. Among his man-
uscripts in Washington's Georgetown University Library are articles on
life in pre-World War I Germany; hand-drawn maps of troop movements
in the Russo-Japanese War; drafts and notes for short stories, plays, movie
scripts, and an unpublished autobiography.*[9]

Emerson was raring to go, so we started out and circled the
mountain and came out on the opposite side. There was just a
scattering of mango trees around the mountain and one could
see for quite a distance. We saw a picket line of Spanish horses
down in the lowlands. I knew they were there, for I had seen
them a few days before. We had just reached a good vantage
point when I saw they were being turned loose to go to water.
I told Emerson to stay hidden behind a few large mango
trees and to signal me if the Spanish were close. I was hidden
from the picket line by a deep draw, and the watering place was
also hidden from the picket line. I rode in and cut off about ten
head of horses and circled them around the mountain in a run
and took them up the creek to the west side of the mountain.
As I took the horses down the draw, Emerson came down the
mountain and we both drove the horses on into camp.

When we arrived, nearly everyone in camp who was able to be on their feet were lined up and ready to go to the train. They caught up all those horses, and anyone who could walk led a horse with the sick loaded on its back. The officers furnished their ponies and walked, too.

When we reached the train, we turned all the horses loose, except one flea-bitten gray, and we took him on into Santiago with the officers' horses. When we got to the docks everything was ready to be loaded. We loaded the officers' horses on a small boat and took them out in the bay and put them on the big boat. I was on loading detail and when I got back they were ready to load us on the boat.

We returned to the United States on the ship *Miami*, and it sure didn't take as long to load our men as it did the horses. In a very short time we were steaming out of that bay for home. We had loaded aboard on August 7, and it was about noon August 8, 1898, that we started sailing. Some of the boys said that they would have liked to look over Santiago a bit, and some did get to, but not for very long. It was three miles down the bay before we hit wide-open ocean. The mouth of the bay is very narrow and just room for two large vessels to pass. Here is where Hobson and the other sailors tried to block the mouth of the bay by sinking a ship. It [the *Merrimac*] was turned so that just one ship could go by. We passed it with about four feet to spare.

Many of you have read of the Morro Castle. In Cuba it was about six hundred to eight hundred feet high, built from stone right into the side of the mountain that faces the ocean at the mouth of the bay. Confined there were the heavily imprisoned [security risks] and life-termers. The cells were built back into the mountain. They were like dungeons where no light could get to them, and I was told that many of the prisoners went blind. Some of the cells had chains fastened in the center, and the prisoners' ankle shackles were chained to them. The cells were barren, cold and dark, and the prisoners were unkempt, uncared for and pitiful in the indescribable unsanitary conditions.

Around the castle, cannons were stationed at about every point the eye could see. Looking up from the bay, cannon stared you in the face all the way along. This was as heavily fortified as any place I had ever seen in my life. The guns didn't look so big, but there were plenty of them. The memory of that place has never left me and, as I write this, I can see it as plainly as if it were yesterday. It is something from the past the keeps coming to mind, and it sure left a lasting impression.

While McGinty was mainly impressed by the austere prison conditions that Morro Castle offered, Roosevelt was more taken by its imposing grandeur. After touring it in late July with only Fifth Corps officers, he called it "a splendid relic of a vanquished power and a vanquished age."[10]

As we came out of the mouth of a bay, we felt like we were nearing home. Our ship was headed for Camp Wikoff, Long Island. After we had been out for about two days, it didn't seem like we were getting anywhere. Colonel Roosevelt went down to the engine room to see what was the matter and found the boilers were cold because the firemen were all drunker than hoot owls.

Colonel Roosevelt came up on deck to see if any of the Rough Riders had ever fired an engine. He finally found some that knew a little about it, so he got them down there and they fired up the ship and it was not long until we were underway again.

I would have thought this job had been the captain's problem, but Colonel Roosevelt often took matters like this into his hands. He gave orders that there would be no more drinking and called the officers together to have them search the ship for liquor and rum. They did it in a nice way, and I guess they got all of it, for I never saw any more men drunk.

After they searched the ship, Colonel Roosevelt explained to the men, using his favorite word of "bully," how things would work from then on. He said, "Bully, we have the liquor now, and from now on I'll be bartender on this ship. If you men really need a drink, come to me and if I think you need it, I'll give it to you." There were some that went to him, too, and I guess he gave them just what they wanted to drink.

The Rough Riders and a squadron of the Third Cavalry regulars shared the transport Miami, *and General Joe Wheeler assigned Roosevelt to manage and oversee policing of the vessel. In a search that Roosevelt personally helped conduct, about seventy flasks and bottles of liquor were confiscated. Roosevelt later wrote that the drunkenness ended abruptly but the below decks crew remained "sullen and half mutinous" and had to be watched.*[11]

The next thing that happened at sea was a death. It was about two o'clock in the morning and it was right near where I was sleeping. I had tied my hammock up high, and after the fellow had passed away, they covered him and brought him over on a cot and put him right under my hammock. I don't know why they did this. I asked them why, and Colonel Roosevelt and Chaplain Brown, who carried him over, told me, "He won't hurt you, McGinty."

The next morning they wrapped the poor fellow in several layers of thick tarp and tied the ends good and tight. Then they tied some iron to his feet. It looked like the iron came from the old grates in the furnace. After the body had been made ready for this type of burial, they carried him to the edge of the deck and slid him feet first overboard. Colonel Roosevelt stood at salute while the body slid into its watery grave. They told me that burial was necessary at sea, for they were not allowed to carry him aboard ship.

The trooper buried at sea was forty-three-year-old George Walsh of San Francisco. The first night ashore in Daiquiri he had gotten drunk

*on rum bartered from the Cubans, and during the next day's march to
Siboney he became violently ill with dysentery and never recovered. His
body, sewn in a hammock weighted with iron shot, was slipped into the
sea off the north coast of Cuba while Third Cavalry band members
played a funeral dirge.*[12]

It seemed like it took quite awhile for us to make the trip
from Cuba to Long Island, but it was only seven days before we
arrived at Montauk Point, Long Island. When we came within
about five miles of shore, a big yacht came out and we were told
that the health officer would be out the next day to inspect us
and decide whether we could land or be held at quarantine.

That gave a lot of us a rather strange feeling as we didn't
know but what we would have to lie out there at anchor for several days. The quarantines were often from thirty to sixty days
and that sure did worry us. There wasn't a boy there that didn't
want to set foot on the soil of the good old United States again
and right away.

That was one place where a person experiences his real love
for his country. There we were, almost home and wanting to
get ashore as soon as we could. The boys were adventurous and
loved traveling, but they loved their home and country, too.
Being back in the United States is what I wanted most. There
is no place in the world like it and its people, and I have traveled over a few countries since those days in Cuba.

It was hard to sit out there and not be able to go ashore. The
doctor on our ship came around next morning before the
health officer showed up, and put the fear in the boys by telling
them if they weren't on their toes and in apparent good health,
that they would be held up for some time. Everything had to
show up good for the health officer to pass us, and it was some
job for a few of those sick soldiers, too. Before the inspection,
we were pretty well organized. An officer preceded the doctor,
and the sickest soldiers were standing up pretty good by the
time he came along, but some were placed where the doctor
never saw them.

This made for a different looking bunch of boys and they all answered "Okay" when the doctor went up to them. He would step up to you and grab your eyelids and pull them open wide and go over you plenty quick, but the eyelids were given the closest inspection. There was a feeling of real joy that spread over that old rolling ship when we found that we could land.

Long Island was a beautiful spot at any time of day, but on this day it seemed even more beautiful. It was only two miles across at the point where we landed. We went on shore at Camp Wikoff, about five miles from the Henlopen lighthouse. The lighthouse was on the south side of the island from us and farther out towards the point of the island. From there it was only a short distance to the east end of the island. We walked about two miles from where we landed and made camp. There were rolling hills with grass that stood about a foot high making a very pretty picture. Here is where we met up again with our saddle horses. They had all been brought up from the south where they earlier had been turned over to the boys that were left behind in Tampa to fight flies, instead of going over to fight Spaniards.

The Miami *dropped anchor off Montauk Point on August 14 and was greeted by a gunboat that carried the news that the Eighth Army Corps had forced the surrender of Manila, essentially ending the war with Spain in the Philippines.*

At noon the next day, the ship tied up at Montauk Pier. General Joe Wheeler led his troops down the gangplank where a large crowd greeted the Rough Riders with "tumultuous cheering and loud shouts of 'Welcome home.'" However, a front-page story in the New York Times *lamented, "The Rough Riders were in too wretched condition to substantially appreciate the noisy greetings. . . . It was all they could do to drag themselves along the road to the point of assembly."*

General S. B. M. Young, by then recovered after being felled by fever, assumed command of Camp Wikoff, which was named in honor of Colonel Charles A. Wikoff, killed in action at El Caney on July 1. The troops who had been left behind in Tampa, Florida, soon joined the returning Cuban veterans at the camp.[13]

There were many ponies here and it was a great place for them. It was good pasture and some of the horses were turned loose to roam the area that contained no timber or settlements. Over closer to New York City, however, there was some timber and more sandy country, too.

While we were there, some of the boys rode their horses down to the ocean and out on the long stretch of beach left when the tide was out; then when the tide started back in, they'd ride the horses back in with it. We all had a lot of fun with this sport, but a sad thing happened there, too. I was down by the ocean one evening at the place where the boys went swimming. There was no one around at this time because when the tide started out, the boys would head back for camp. I was riding up along the sand and there on the shore I saw two little piles of clothing. I didn't pay much attention to it at the time, for I just figured it was discarded clothing, so I rode on back to camp and never thought much more about it.

An hour or so later I heard some of the boys talking about General Wheeler's son and another officer's son who had disappeared and no one knew what had happened to them. They said that they thought the boys had gone swimming that afternoon while the tide was in, and I happened to think of those two piles of clothing. I went to some of the officers and told them about the clothing piled on the beach, and they asked me to go show them, but we all knew by then what had happened to them.

When we got there, their clothing was lying in the same place. The officers looked it over and found it did belong to the missing boys. They had stayed in too long and when the tide started out they had been carried out to sea. No one knew what to do, so we went up to the lighthouse to ask them about recovering the bodies. The men at the lighthouse told us that about all we could do was wait. They said that between 12:00 and 1:00 A.M., the tide would come in, and the bodies would be carried to shore then. They also told us that the drift of the ocean would carry the bodies about a half mile east from where they had gone in.

Late that night quite a bunch of us went down to about a half mile from where the boys were swimming. Sure enough, when the tide came in, it brought the bodies to nearly the same spot the lighthouse men told us. Some of the men said that they came in together while others said they were just near each other, but I wasn't at the spot when they found them and the bodies were carried away before I got there.

CHAPTER 4

Footloose and Free

MY captain, as I have before mentioned, was Captain Woodbury Kane, really a swell fellow. He was a great sailor and a few years before the war had won some sailing races in England. I found out after our return to the states that he had sailed all over the world and was well known in the East for his sailing exploits.

He was given considerable honor upon our return and had many high-powered friends. He came to me one day at Camp Wikoff and told me that he would like for me to be orderly to Colonel Roosevelt and himself at a dinner over on the island. He was worried a bit about their horses, for he knew there was to be a large number at the dinner and didn't know where they could leave the horses. I told him that I would look after them.

We left headquarters' camp the next night after dark, and there was no road or trail to follow, just small rolling hills and prairie glades. They told me that it was about a five-mile ride, and after a time we saw a big house in the distance all lit up, and Colonel Roosevelt remarked that this was the place. I wondered at the time how he knew, but later found out that this was the only house or any kind of settlement on that part of the island.

When we arrived, Colonel Roosevelt and Captain Kane dismounted and waited around a bit until someone came out of the house and showed them in. I made the horses fast, and went on up to the house. There were several important officers there, all dressed in their military best. They sure made a sight with buttons and insignias shining, so that it near dimmed the brilliance of the bright chandeliers that lit the rooms. The dining room was centered with a huge banquet table, the longest that I had ever seen, and the bright chinaware and the silverware was really something to look at.

A great many officers in those days wore a mustache, and that seemed a mark of rank in the room that night. Before dinner was called, the officers were all congregated in a big reception hall and waiting room, and when they marched into dinner and lined up at the table, it looked very military-like, almost as if they had drilled and practiced for the occasion. I was in the next room watching through the doors between the rooms that were made of full-length glass. Naturally I wished that I was inside at that banquet table, and as I watched them there, I wished, too, that I had the training and military precision of those men. But with only the rough education of a cowboy on the ranges of Oklahoma, I still felt flattered that I had been picked to accompany these men as their orderly.

I got to talking to one of the waitresses who had known Captain Kane for many years, and when I told her that I was with the captain, she sure did treat me fine. We all ate in the kitchen, and the officers never had us bested any on food because we had everything in the back room that they had on the banquet table. There were meats and vegetables of all kinds, topped off with wine courses, the best that money could afford. There were three women in the kitchen; one was an English girl that I remember well, for she talked so fast and in such broken English that I could hardly understand her. She was a rather pretty girl, too.

The party broke up about one o'clock. When we had started for the banquet the moon was up, but before we started back it had gone down and it was really dark. During dinner I had been watching to see General Shafter, but he was not there. I guess he wasn't invited or something because no one seemed greatly interested in him, even though he had been a big shot in Cuba. He was big all other ways, too, about the size of screen comedian Fatty Arbuckle of the early cinema days.

William McKinley was president during this time, and
shortly after we landed he came over to the island to review the
troops. I guess he wanted to see how we looked after returning from Cuba. The officers had us all lined up at attention on
horseback, and President McKinley came down the line riding
in a fine-looking carriage drawn by some dandy white horses.
The carriage had big sidelights on it, and they were all shined
up. They looked somewhat like the old brass lamps that came
out on the early-day Fords. We had been lectured on just how
to act and how to be at attention and I thought we all did fairly
well.

President McKinley, along with the vice president, secretary of war,
and other cabinet members, visited the camp on September 3. After his
speechmaking and inspection of the troops, McKinley visited General
Shafter, who was still confined in the camp hospital with malaria.[1]

A few days after the president had reviewed the troops, word
got around that anyone that wasn't in good physical shape
would be taken to a hospital and held there until he was fully
recovered. Everyone was more interested in getting mustered
out, so men didn't want to hang around a hospital. The main
subject was getting our discharge, so when the inspecting
officers came around, and said, "How are you?" everyone
answered, "I'm fit as a fiddle, nothing wrong with me." They
knew a lot of them were not telling the truth and I wasn't
either, but I sure didn't want to hang around a hospital. Some
of them said that if you went to the hospital you might be held
over and not discharged and then when you got well you might
be thrown in the regular army. I had no desire for either, and I
knew I would never make the grade in the regulars.

There was one of the boys in our troop named Charley
Knoblauck [sometimes Knoblauch], and he had been on the
Stock Exchange in New York City at the time of his enlist-
ment. He got leave and went over to the city and he must have

told them at the Stock Exchange that some of the boys needed special food because the people in New York City chipped in and sent wagon loads of oranges and other fruits and vegetables to the island. It was food that we really needed too, and we didn't have to sign up to get it, it was just dished out. I will say one thing for those people on the Stock Exchange, they really treated us swell, and Charley Knoblauck told us, "Boys if there is anything of any kind that you want to eat, name it and we'll get it." Charley Knoblauck is on the Stock Exchange at this time [late 1930s] and I consider him among my great friends.

One day while we were in camp, two of Teddy Roosevelt's boys came down to headquarters. They were around fourteen and eighteen years of age at that time, and Colonel Roosevelt asked me to pick them out some good horses to ride, and he didn't say anything about being gentle ones either. He also asked me to show them around a bit. I got the boys some good horses with plenty of spirit as they both were excellent horsemen. There was a dun-colored horse in the bunch that was loose on the island and I had wanted to catch him. I figured I might be able to get the horse with the help of the Roosevelt boys. They were more than willing after I told them about it, so we rode down around a little nook on the island. We finally found the pony on a patch of land that ran out into the ocean, so we drove him down along this bottleneck of land.

I told the boys to run the pony out past me and I would rope him. They started running the pony up the waterfront and I was laying for him. When he got close, I started crowding him a bit with my swinging rope and kept right after him and he finally jumped off in the water and mud. The colonel's boys were scared and got to wondering what to do. I was afraid the mud would suck the horse down and drown him, but while he was trying to get up I got my rope on him. I tied the rope to the regulation government saddle that I was using, and finally upset the horse and pulled him out on his back.

We were all sure glad to get that pony out and led him back to camp. Coming near camp, we saw a big bunch of people ganged around Teddy Roosevelt's tent and one of the boys, noticing the group, turned to me and remarked, "I hope to be as great a man as my father some day."

The boys stayed around camp for several days and seemed to have quite a time. They were anxious to see their father's horse, "Little Tex," of which their dad was so proud. The horses, however, were hard to find because so many of them had been loose on the island. The ones that had been in Cuba were turned out with a number that had not been sent over, and a man who didn't know brands or horses very well would have a hard time finding any one horse in the bunch.

The Roosevelt boys who visited camp were eleven-year-old Theodore, Jr., and nine-year-old Kermit. Both later served in World Wars One and Two and were said to be as aggressive in soldiering as their father. Kermit Roosevelt, who was given to hard-drinking and living, killed himself while on active duty at Fort Richardson, Alaska, in 1943. On D-Day in 1944, Brigadier General Theodore Roosevelt, Jr., led some of the first troops ashore at Normandy and was awarded the Medal of Honor for gallantry. He died of a heart attack a few weeks later.[2]

One day I happened to be near Colonel Roosevelt and he called to me and asked, "McGinty, do you think you could find my horse, Little Tex?" "Yes sir, Colonel," I replied. Then he told me, "McGinty, I am going to detail you to find Little Tex, for I've had a man looking for him for several days and he hasn't found him yet."

I got to figuring that if that fellow had been looking for the horse among the loose ones on the island and hadn't found him, then he might be on the regular picket line. I looked over all the picket lines but couldn't find him, so I started prowling around the island among the loose horses and finally located him.

I took "Little Tex" to the picket line and he stayed there until we were mustered out. A short time after that, I saw Major Jenkins one day and he said, "McGinty, I am going to give you that horse you bought for me in Texas before we went to Cuba." The horse was really a good one and I sure did thank the major for him. He was one fine fellow and we had known many of the same people of the Old West.

The horse the major gave me had gotten away from the headquarters picket line and had been tied on the regulars' line. I went over to get him, but the guard wouldn't let me have the horse. I then went to the major and told him about it. He was lying down at the time [but] jumped up and said that he would go with me and we would get him.

The major and I walked over to the picket line, which was about a half-mile away, but the guard wouldn't let him have his own horse. The guard told us that the horse had been on the picket line when he came on duty, and he was going to stay there until an order came to let him go. Major Jenkins told him, "We'll get him alright," so we walked over to Colonel Roosevelt's tent.

We told Teddy our troubles, and he asked where the line was. We told him it was quite a walk, but he said he would get the horse for us. So we all three walked back to the picket. When we got there the colonel asked us which horse it was, and after I pointed him out, Teddy walked up to the picket line past the guard, untied the horse and led him out to us, and handed the lead rope to me. The colonel never said a word to the guard, nor did the guard to him. The colonel seemed to have a different way of going about things than we did. There was another thing too, his ways worked and ours didn't.

After approximately one month on Long Island, the Rough Riders began the mustering out process on September 13. That afternoon the entire regiment formed near Roosevelt's tent, at which time officers requested the colonel's presence. On a table in the center of the

*formation sat a bulky object covered by a blanket. There, Private
William S. Murphy, a Troop M volunteer from Caddo, Indian Territory, had the honor of presenting Roosevelt a bronze sculpture of a cowboy on a bucking horse, the work of Frederic Remington, who had served
as a correspondent-artist in the Cuban campaign. Roosevelt, never at a
loss for words, said he was "proud of this regiment beyond measure"
especially the "backbone" of it, "the men of the West and Southwest."
The remainder of that night and the next, Roosevelt later recalled, was
spent in noisy, harmless hilarity.*

*On September 15, 1898, only four months after its formation in San
Antonio, the Rough Riders' regimental colors were lowered for the last
time. In just over a week of actual fighting, they had been part of a force
that ended four hundred years of Spanish reign in Cuba. In doing so, the
First United States Volunteer Cavalry had suffered a thirty-seven percent
loss in men killed, wounded, or stricken with disease. In the Treaty of
Paris, signed December 10, 1898, Spain relinquished sovereignty over
Cuba and ceded Puerto Rico, Guam, and the Mariana Islands to the
United States. For a twenty-million-dollar payment, Spain also gave up
the Philippines, where, before the fighting in Cuba began, Commodore
George Dewey had fired the first shots of the Spanish-American War in
the brief and victorious battle of Manila Bay on May 1, 1898, earning
him national fame and promotion to admiral. Ultimately, however, the
American occupation of the Philippines as a colonial possession led to
new hostilities with the Filipino population. Thousands of American
troops then shipped out to fight in that long and costly conflict, which
finally ended in July 1902 after U.S. battlefield losses of over four thousand dead and nearly three thousand wounded.*[3]

After we were mustered out, Colonel Roosevelt asked me to
bring his pony down to his home at Oyster Bay. Oyster Bay was
about one hundred miles down the island and two of the boys,
William Quade and George Knoblauck, went with me. There
was another fellow, William Buckle, who started with us, but I
guess we weren't going fast enough for him, so he rode off and
left us.

Roosevelt bids farewell to each Rough Rider at Camp Wikoff. The Frederic Remington Statue of a cowboy on a bucking horse stands on the table behind him. Courtesy of Bartleby.com, Inc. © 1997.

After riding down the island for about twenty-five miles, we came upon some settlements and little towns. It seemed that the people along the way knew I was bringing "Little Tex" for they lined up along the way and ganged around the little horse. They all had a great admiration for Teddy Roosevelt and even cheered his horse as if it were human, but they were not human in their actions to the pony. People would come up and pat the horse and then pull some of the hairs from his tail and mane to keep for souvenirs.

When we reached Colonel Roosevelt's home, Sagamore Hill, which was about four miles from Oyster Bay, I took the horse up to the east side of the house. Mrs. Roosevelt came out first, and then Alice, followed by the colonel. Teddy looked

"Little Tex" over and I noticed he was looking mostly at his tail and mane when he remarked, "Well, 'Little Tex' don't look much like himself, what's wrong?" I told him that I didn't know, for I fed him well along the way.

I never told him what had really happened, but Teddy kept on talking and I knew he wanted to know, but I never did tell him that people along the way had nearly pulled all his mane and tail out to keep for souvenirs. The pony looked pretty bad; as if the calves had been a hold of his tail and had chewed it off. Anyway, I never did think much of the pony as a saddle horse but I guess he was a pretty good cavalry horse. Mrs. Roosevelt called a "darky" to take "Little Tex" around to the stables; then she turned to me to say that he would be well cared for the rest of his life.

George Knoblauck, William Quade, and I then rode back to camp and on into New York City. That was my first visit to the big town. I was riding the horse that the Major gave me, so I took him over to the livery stable and then went out to do the town. I met one of the troopers in the city, who told me that an auction was to be held for some of the Rough Riders' horses and that he wanted me to buy a certain one for him. I later went up to the auction and just as I got there they were selling the horse this fellow wanted. Some were bidding on him, but before I could open my mouth, the auctioneer hollered out, "Sold." I later sold my own horse for thirty dollars. I would have liked to keep him but didn't have any place there to use a horse much.

George Knoblauck and I were staying at the Morton Hotel, which was at Thirteenth and Broadway. George left after a few days but I stayed on for a while. During my first days in New York City I really took in the town. While I was out one day I thought I would walk back to the hotel. I walked and walked until I was about all fagged out, and then I must be lost or the hotel was, so I stopped a taxicab and told him to take me to the hotel. He circled the block and there it was on the next street.

There was a fellow staying at the same hotel named Paige. He was an actor and working in rehearsal for a play that was to be called the "Battle of All Nations." Now, to fully understand the feelings of those times, I want to explain how people expressed themselves on the stage and in newspapers. As in any war, emotions ran high and any patriotic theme was highly successful. The public rejoiced over the victories and the returning soldiers were heroes, so the trend in the theatre was to portray war heroes and have all the well-known fighters and officers of the war present, if possible. The public ate this stuff up, too, and there was great interest in that type of stage show or story.

We had a fellow in our regiment who had been a great speaker and orator before going to Cuba, and on his return he went immediately to the stage and lecture hall and made big money for his war stories and adventures. For this reason, the show "Battle of All Nations" was in hurried rehearsal. One day Paige asked me to come up to the theatre where they were learning their parts, and try out. I was a bit leery about going because I did not have any stage experience. It all was a deep mystery to me and pretty scary for a poor cowboy who knew very little about anything except horses and western trails.

Finally, I got up enough nerve to go and they sure were busy rushing about here and there. I just stood off to one side, looking wide-eyed and wondering what they were trying to do, and why they were rushing about so much. Finally, a fellow came up to me who acted like he was the boss or something. He told me, "Get on the outside, young man, we're busy in here." He had a look that let a fellow know he meant it, too. He came at me so sharp and so crabby-like that I came near turning around and beating it, but I told him, "I got a friend in here that I want to see."

He snapped back at me, "This is no place to visit your friends. We're busy so get out." It finally dawned on me that I should tell him about Paige and who I was. When I did, he acted a little bit better. He told me to follow him and he took me over by the stage and asked me if I could ride a horse and handle a gun and saber all at the same time. I told him I thought I could, and he asked me if I wanted to join up with the show. I told him that I would make a stab at it and he said he would find out if I would do.

I soon learned that I was to play the part of General Joe Wheeler, who was also a small man about my size. They fixed me a wig, some makeup, and a costume, then gave me a horse and a saber and gun. The director then showed me how to salute with the sabers, all in military precision. He also showed me a few tricks with the six-gun. I could do this all right for I had seen it done many times, but this wasn't the acting part. When it came to really acting it was my first experience at it and, boy-e-e, I guess I was greener than green, even though I didn't think so at the time. When I had gone through the action a few times, the boss said, "McGinty put some force into the acting! Do it a bit faster and show by your face that you mean it. You're not earnest enough in action."

He put another fellow on the horse and showed me what he meant. The other fellow had rehearsed for the part and had all the acting right, but no ability with the horse and gun. After the fellow showed me through the part, he put me back on the horse and I tried it myself. I knew that I was just going through the motions, and it looked like I never could get it just like he wanted. He kept telling me over and over, "McGinty, put some life in it, make yourself think it is the real thing and that you really are General Joe Wheeler." Paige tried to help me, too, and they sure got mad, but I was dumb and never knew a thing about this acting business anyway.

Finally, the boss threw up his hands, and said he couldn't use me. What he really meant was that he could never teach me to act, but I didn't care for it much anyway because it didn't look too good to me. They kept bawling out all the folks who were trying to act and that bawling-out stuff didn't set well with me.

I finally left and went back to the hotel and sat around until Paige came home from rehearsing. When he arrived he just busted out laughing and really gavè me the hee-haw. He stopped long enough to ask me how I liked the director, and I told him that he acted too hard-boiled for me, and that I was sorry that I even went up there. Paige told me that I should have explained to the director who I was and that I had no acting experience, then he would probably have been a bit easier on me.

Paige told me to forget the whole matter and to return to the theatre the next morning. That night he asked me up to his room for supper. It turned out to be one of the greatest lessons of my life. It had to do with acting and Paige was one of the most considerate and nicest fellows that I had ever met. He tried to give me every bit of the experience that he gained as an actor. He showed me how to change my facial expression and had me practice it. He also gave me pointers on carriage and actions of my body and how to keep an alert and poised acting expression. He told me what to do with my hands and feet to keep them at ease, how to forget stage fright, and how to avoid getting mad from being bawled out.

There in that room in the Morton Hotel, nearly all night through, I sat and listened as I had never done before, and when I went to bed in the early morning hours, my eyes were red with want of sleep, and my mind was so full of things that I could hardly rest.

Early the next morning Paige and I went to the theatre. There on the stage before anyone else appeared he went over my part with me. After a while the director came in and he never spoke a word to us. We were busy and just went on working. He went out in the seats and sat down waiting for the others to get there and, after I had gone over part of my act for what seemed the hundredth time that morning, he came up on the stage.

The director had a kind of rough voice anyway and he looked at Paige and said, "Maybe you had better take my job as instructor." I thought he was mad, and I guess Paige did, too, because he told him, "I am sorry that you take it this way. I was not trying to be smart but was just trying to show McGinty a few things."

The director then told him that he meant it as a compliment and thought that he had really done a good job of instructing. He then said that he figured he could use me now, but that it would still take a lot of practicing. I came back the next morning and I got a new pair of spurs and felt a lot better. I really put the horse through some action and fairly cut a swath with the saber. From then on the part went along all right and it finally came time for the show to open.

This first show of my life was both a scary and thrilling experience to me. The part I played was helpful because General Joe Wheeler was well liked by the North and South. He had been a hero in the Civil War as well as the Spanish-American War. The show was heralded a great success, and while it probably would not be much today, the public in those days, especially in New York City, seemed hungry for any kind of war story or show.

Even though I knew little about show business, the play's success sure made me feel good. I was getting a lot of cheers for my acting and thought they were for me until I realized they were really only cheering for who I was supposed to be, General Joe Wheeler. Even so, the cheering made me feel good.

One evening while I was sitting on my pony waiting for my turn to go on, I had my six-shooter in my hand and was twirling it on my finger. The director happened to go by about that time, and he stopped and said, "Let's see you do that again." I did it for him and he asked if I could twirl the gun and fire it every time it came around. I told him that I could, so he asked me to report early the next morning and we would go over a new part for the act.

As the show continued, the fellow that originally had my part kept right on working. He was what was called my understudy and I guess he got paid the same as me. Anyway, it was a good thing they had the fellow, because after the show played for several weeks I caught a spell of fever and chills as an aftermath of the war and was taken to a hospital in New York City.

The doctor examined me and told me that the city did not agree with me and I would have to leave for a change of climate. Before going to the hospital I was real sick and stayed in the hotel room. I had Paige get me some medicine, but I had the chills so bad that I would nearly shake the bed down, and sometimes the fever would feel like it was burning me up. I tried to get some old-fashioned chill medicine like we used for malaria in Oklahoma, but those New York folks didn't seem to know what it was. Somehow my captain, Woodbury Kane, found out I was sick, so he came over to the hotel and told me I should go back to the hospital. I sure didn't want to go, but he kept after me until I finally went.

The captain dispelled my fears of the hospital by telling me that he had a friend there and he knew they would give me fine treatment. I did get good treatment and the nurses and doctors were very kind. It was the Roosevelt Hospital, and was a dandy place all right, but I was my own boss and could do as I pleased.

The remarkable friendship between New Yorker Woodbury Kane and Billy continued for some time after the war. Kane, a cousin to John Jacob Astor, had been a close friend of Roosevelt when they attended Harvard many years earlier. In spite of his wealth and notoriety as a "blooded" aristocrat, Kane was easily the most down-to-earth member of the "Fifth Avenue Boys." When the war started, he wanted only to serve and joined as a trooper. Roosevelt recalled seeing him on kitchen duty at camp in San Antonio, but before leaving Texas, Roosevelt personally appointed Kane a lieutenant in Troop K, saying he had "won his commission" through hard work and leadership. On the battlefield in Cuba, Kane was promoted to captain.[4]

After I had been in the hospital for about five days, I felt much better, so I asked for a pass to go downtown for awhile.

I think the passes they issued were good for two hours, but when I left I knew that I had no intention of returning to that place. I got a pass and left the hospital and went back over to the rooming house and rented a room. Then I wandered around town a bit.

Along toward evening I began feeling rather sick and weak, so I started back for my room. By the time I got there, my fever was pretty high again, and I was real sick. I had quite a chill and really needed a doctor, so they called one from the rooming house, and I asked them to call the same doctor that had looked after me before I went to the hospital.

When he came and looked me over, he told me, "Young man, there is nothing I can do for you." I sure thought I had played thunder by leaving the hospital. I asked the doctor what was wrong with me, and he went on to explain to me again that on account of my health that I must leave New York City. The climate was not suited to me or I to the climate, I guess. Anyway, the way he explained it was that in my sickly condition I should not stay in New York City. Meanwhile, Captain Kane had been informed that I had skipped out from the hospital, so he came around to look me up again.

It was like that in those days. The captain had no responsibility in such cases as mine because we had already been turned loose from the army but he was a fine fellow and kept up with us boys and looked after us, especially the boys who had been under his command. My condition was a result of the war and, like many others, I was weak due to the poison and fever in my system that was brought back from Cuba. It was called "tropical fever" and many who have been in the jungles and tropical climates of the world have experienced such a malady, and can well realize that it is much like the chills and fever of malaria.

I told the captain what the doctor had told me about leaving New York for my health. He said that this would work in fine with some plans he had since he was planning a trip to Pine Island, Florida, with some of the fellows to do some tarpon fishing. When he asked me to go along with them I could hardly believe it. It was a rather big invitation for a plain trooper and I didn't know how to take it. There was Captain Kane, a millionaire, along with his rich friends, and me, a poor sick cowboy, more of a burden than anything else. Of course I accepted and a few days later we left.

There were four of us in the party that made the trip, and although I was a bit sick, I made the trip down there okay. When we reached Pine Island, Florida, I thought I would ask about getting some chill tonic, because we were in a place where they knew what chill tonic was, and sure enough the druggist had some. He told me that a couple of bottles should straighten me out, so I bought two bottles of the stuff. Most of you know just how bitter that old-fashioned chill tonic was but it sure did the trick. It pulled me right out of the kinks in no time.

The captain and his friends went out fishing every day and I went along for the sport, although it was something I didn't know much about. They had a yacht and would lead a smaller boat behind it. When they reached the point they wanted to fish they had a man from Pine Island who took the yacht back to the small town on the Island, and then return to get us later in the evening.

This tarpon fishing was really some sport to those fellows. They sat out there all day long in that hot sun and their faces would get red and the skin peeled off until they really looked a sight. The reflection of the sun on the water makes it much worse to burn and one day, after I had been out in an extremely hot sun, my face blistered, peeled, and burned like a red hot fire all night long.

A tarpon is quite a game fish and a real fighter and once one was hooked he would float up to the surface of the water, flounce around a bit, and then high-tail it away. The men used extra heavy lines with reels that had brakes on them. They would let the tarpon out a ways until he slowed up some, and then they would reel him in close. When the tarpon got close enough to see the boat, then away he would go again and the heavy lines would whine and sing. The captain and others then braced their feet in chairs by the small rails and whip back on the rod, then get a hold on the reel brakes and let out the line.

They told me that an average tarpon weighed around one hundred pounds and that they had to run him three or four times before they could get him even close to the boat. Once the fish was worn down, they reeled him in close to the boat and either shot him or knocked him in the head. They then dragged him aboard, and everyone would stand around looking him over. Then, with a big smile on their faces they would say that he sure was a big one and sure did put up a big fight.

This might have been real sport but not for me. I liked to fish some, but I liked to rope bulls and wild cattle even better, and let them run on the rope and give them a turn over. Tarpon fishing may have been the same sort of thing to them because they claimed the tarpon was really a fighter, and just as in roping wild horses or bulls, you get a bigger kick out of it if they have some life in them.

When we got back to shore with the fish, they would drag their catch off, then hang them up and weigh and measure them. I suppose that when they got back to New York City the fish had grown some, but here they averaged from one hundred to one hundred twenty-five pounds and were about five feet in length. Afterwards they cut off about ten pounds of meat from the tarpon's back, what they called tenderloin. The meat was good and real white in color. The scales on those tarpon are about as big as a half saucer. Here, too, was the first time I knew that salt-water catfish were not good to eat. They were considered a scavenger fish and the natives would no more eat them than they would a snake. It was near here, along the Gulf of Mexico, that during the Spanish-American War, the cable to Cuba was cut.

The cutting of the cables at Cienfuegos, Cuba, was one of the most remarkable events of the Spanish-American War. While the American

Navy's blockade of the entire Cuban coast prevented the landing of food supplies and munitions, Spanish commanders still maintained direct communication, via underwater telegraph cables, with the islands of the West Indies and, thus, with the home government at Madrid. Cutting the cables and destroying all lines of communication became of utmost strategic importance.

On May 11, 1898, volunteer navy blue jackets and marines from the cruiser USS Marblehead and gunboat USS Nashville went ashore in small launches at Cienfuegos on Cuba's southern coast, the key point where the cables came inland. Under intense enemy fire, the Americans dredged up and cut the important underwater cables that linked the military forces at Cienfuegos with its commanders and the rest of the world. Fifty-two Medals of Honor were awarded for the heroic action that day.

While an undersea cable from the United States extended to Cuba from the Florida Gulf Coast where Billy went fishing after the war, communication on that cable was controlled by the U.S. and, thus, it was never necessary to sever it.[5]

Before we left Pine Island, Captain Kane asked me how I would like to start a cow ranch in Cuba. There was quite a need for beef in Cuba, where cows were mighty scarce and high in price. He figured that we could buy them cheap, and since shipping was not too expensive, could sell them at a good price and make some money.

I looked around a bit to see what we could buy cattle for in that part of Florida. There were many cattle around all right, but after looking them over, they seemed rather knotty to me and they only weighed around five hundred pounds. I found out that I could buy all I wanted for around six dollars a head. At the time, cows were selling for around thirty to thirty-five a head in the West.

Cattle were so high in Cuba and there were so few of them that it seemed like quite a moneymaking proposition to buy them and ship them across. Captain Kane told me that he would go up to Washington and find out what kind of business prospects there were in Cuba and what our foreign relations would be. I waited in Florida and after several days he sent me a wire saying that after checking things over the venture would not be very safe, so we dropped it.

After getting the wire I decided to return to New York City. Teddy Roosevelt was running for governor and I kind of wanted to be around. Teddy was running on the Republican ticket and a fellow named Mark Hanna was his campaign manager. Hanna was a fellow that sure could get a lot of work done for one man. I met him on a few different occasions and was much impressed with his ability as an organizer and manager. He seemed to be on the go every minute, always doing a bunch of different things at the same time. He was a great politician as well as journalist.

Because I was greatly interested in this election, I rented a room close to downtown on Thirteenth Street, where Fifth Avenue meets Broadway. I had a good view down Broadway and could watch the big signs that flashed out the news and the returns on election night.

I remember election night as plainly as if it were yesterday. The first returns came in from the city precincts and were very disheartening because the city was mostly Democrat. They gave Teddy's opponent on the Democrat ticket [Augustus Van Wyck] a big lead. I lay there on the bed watching those flashes and each time it looked more and more as if Teddy had lost. I felt a bit sad because he was as close to me as any friend could be and his loss was my loss. I finally dozed off to sleep and it was well after midnight when I was awakened by a news butch crying below my window. He was hollering, "Extra, Roosevelt wins Governorship." So I looked again at the sign and the next time it flashed, sure enough Teddy was in the lead.

I hurried out of the hotel onto the street and when I reached the street level there was only one way a person could go and that was with the direction of the crowd. It seemed that everyone in New York City was marching in a big parade for Teddy Roosevelt's triumph. They were going down the street chanting and singing, with their hands on each other's shoulders. They were in a snake dance formation from Thirteenth and Broadway to the Flat Iron Building, then across East to Fifth Avenue, and back down Fifth Avenue to Thirteenth Street. This took the crowd clear around the place where they were flashing the election returns. I joined in the parade and it was some wild bunch, and we certainly did celebrate that night.

A few days after Teddy's election, I saw Captain Kane again and he asked me to go to the upper part of the New York State to look after some polo ponies he had. He was hoping I would stay there and work for him, but I told the captain that I would rather go back to Indian Territory. When he saw I was a bit homesick for Oklahoma and didn't want to go up there for him, he told me that his sister was interested in starting me out in the cattle business in the West if I wanted to go back. He wanted to know if I knew of a good cow ranch that we could buy out. I told him that the cattle business was a lot like other businesses, and that it sometimes had its up and downs. I explained that because cattle were high in the West, that it was not too good a proposition for her. I thanked him very much for his interest and his sister's kind offer and told him that I thought I would just wander around and see what I could get in work and that I would get along all right.

While we were talking it over, we were sitting in the Knicker-bocker Club, a very ritzy place whose members were very rich men. We sat there talking in those big easy chairs and Captain Kane sat back and just looked at me after I had told him I wouldn't accept his sister's offer. Finally he said, "McGinty, don't be foolish, my sister really would get a pleasure, as well as I, out of this kind of venture and I would greatly appreciate you accepting it."

I thought this over for a little while because, after all, he was very kind in helping me, so I told him that I had a little money and would go back to Indian Territory and look around. Then after seeing how things looked, I would drop him a line and if his sister still desired to stake me, it would be all right. Captain Kane asked me to come back to the club later in the evening after he had time to talk to his sister and explain how I had reacted.

I returned to the club later that evening and he was waiting for me. We ordered dinner and while we sat there eating, we talked of the West and of early days on the range. He told me that he had a brother buried in Arizona, and this was the first time that he had ever mentioned this to me. He said that the West was very deeply etched in his mind and that as a remembrance to his brother, he and his sister would appreciate helping me, and my accepting, because it was a token of feeling and remembrance for him. He felt that they were a part in the building of the West as an empire and that by helping me he was keeping the memory of his brother alive. When I went to leave he handed me a piece of paper and after I had left the club I looked at it and saw it was a check for one thousand dollars.

I took the check and came back to home and Oklahoma, arriving in Perry and then at Ingalls. I stayed around Ingalls a few days visiting old friends, and then went over near Bristow in Indian Territory, where my brother lived. I told him that I wanted to buy a few cows, and asked him if he knew of anything worth buying.

He told me of a man who lived up on Rock Creek by the name of Skidmore who had some Texas cows and that he wanted to sell out what was left because they were poor and could not go on the market. We went up there and I put some more money with the check and bought him out.

It was near the latter part of January of 1899 when I bought these cattle to make a start as rancher. I bought a lease up on Polecat Creek, which was southwest of Kellyville. This part of the country was known as the Creek Nation. In Indian Territory during those days, a man had to have a lease to hold cattle on it.

After we had moved the cattle over from Rock Creek to Polecat Creek, I left them in care of my brother and returned to
Ingalls. I already had a few horses there and fully intended to
sell them and return to my ranching duties, but a letter I
received while there changed the course of my life for the next
few years.

CHAPTER 5

The Buffalo Bill Show

THE letter came from the booking agent of Buffalo Bill's shows and it read in part, "Mr. Billy McGinty: As Buffalo Bill's shows are adding a new act, 'The Battle of San Juan Hill,' please wire your acceptance of a contract for the year 1899."

That meant a return to New York City, and when I had left I thought at the time I never would return. This was a big decision for me because I had never really liked the acting business, or at least what I had seen of it. My preference was to ride the range and be in the open as my own boss, but a young man's fancy sometimes turns to fame and fortune and I decided to go. Buffalo Bill's show was a bit different than the stage, otherwise I wouldn't have been so interested.

I went back to Polecat Creek and told my brother about the offer. He thought I should go, too, and said he could look after the cattle. After talking it over, I rode into Bristow and wired them that I would accept. In a few days the booking agent wired me a ticket and sent along a train schedule for the route. This was near the middle of February and we were supposed to be in New York City on February 22. A young fellow by the name of Johnny Baker was in charge of the train schedules and show bookings. He figured out the schedules for the foreigners as well as the Americans in the show, and his job was to get everyone to New York in time to start rehearsal on the given date.

I met a few of the boys on the train ride to Chicago, but at the station there I met a bunch more who were with the Rough

Billy McGinty and five Rough Rider friends who joined the Buffalo Bill show after the Spanish-American War. Standing L to R: Roscoe "Ben" Miller, Troop D; Tom Isbell, Troop L. Middle, seated: Sgt. Gerald Webb, Troop D; Fred Beal, Troop D. On floor, L to R: McGinty, Troop K, and Joe Kline, Troop L. Glenn D. Shirley Western Americana Collection, National Cowboy & Western Heritage Museum.

Riders. There was Lon Muxlow of Guthrie, Oklahoma Territory; Sel Newcomb of Waukomis, O.T.; Fred Beal of Kingfisher, O.T.; Tom Isbell and Joe Kline of Vinita, Indian Territory; Tom Holmes of Newkirk, O.T.; Henry Meagher of El Reno, O.T.; Jesse Langdon of Omaha, Nebraska; Bob Ragland and James T. Brown of Los Angeles; G. A. Webb of Nevada; Francis Byrnes of Yuma, Arizona; Walter Cook of Enid, O.T.; Ben and V. D. Miller of Guthrie, O.T.; J. H. Tait of Phoenix; and C. D. Scott of Shawnee, O.T. Of this group, G. A. Webb was sergeant and I was color bearer for the act in the show.

A few of the towns Billy listed as places where his friends resided differ from the Rough Riders' muster rolls, probably because some of the men had moved after the war and prior to joining Buffalo Bill's Wild West show.

Jesse D. Langdon listed his home as Fargo, North Dakota. Robert C.
Ragland enlisted at Guthrie, as did James T. Brown, who was from
Oxford, Kansas. Gerald A. Webb was also originally from Guthrie, and
while no "Francis" Byrnes appears on the muster rolls, there was a Peter
Francis Byrne who joined at Guthrie, as well as John H. Tait from Raton,
New Mexico.[1]

While at the depot in Chicago, I also met a bunch of the cow-
boys I knew who had signed up for cowboy acts with the show.
Of the cowboys I remember, the best known were George
Gardner and Walter Scott. Scott is better known today as
"Death Valley Scotty." With all these boys we had quite a time
on the train from Chicago.

George Gardner and his wife, Ina, joined the show in 1899. The "real
life" Montana cowboy performed as a rodeo contestant and peace officer,
while Ina posed as a cowgirl. After leaving the show in 1906, he went on
to win the "World's Champion Best All-Around Cowboy" honors at the
Glendive (Montana) Roundup in 1919.

At age thirteen, Walter Scott was a "swamper" on a twenty-mule team
driving borax across the Mojave Desert. In 1888 he joined the show as a
stunt rider, touring for twelve years. Not only was Scott a skillful per-
former on stage, he pulled off several "con" schemes back in Death Valley
California, as McGinty later relates.[2]

It was February 22, right on schedule that we arrived at the
Erie depot in Jersey City. If I remember correctly, this was
located at the Twenty Second Street Ferry on the Hudson. We
were met by an agent of the show and taken across the Hudson
through the city to the Brooklyn Bridge. There on the East
River, on the Brooklyn side, was a small plot of ground called
Ambrose Park that lay between the cities on each side. This was
the rehearsal site of Buffalo Bill's shows.

William F. "Buffalo Bill" Cody started his Wild West show as a local
Fourth of July celebration called the "Old Glory Blow Out" near his

North Platte, Nebraska, ranch in 1882. What is considered to be one of the first rodeos in America was so successful that Cody teamed with a promoter and created an outdoor show called the "Rocky Mountain and Prairie Exhibition" in 1883. Under new management the following year, it became "Buffalo Bill's Wild West," the most successful touring show of all time, playing before millions of spectators for more than three decades.

Half circus and half history lesson, the show mixed sentimentality with sensationalism. Images of the romantic, wide-open West were especially well received in the heavily industrialized cities of the East, where the show served to confirm a stereotypical notion of life west of the Mississippi.

In 1893 the show added the title "Congress of Rough Riders of the World" to capitalize on the public's fascination with horses and horsemanship. The show found historical significance when Cody's friend Theodore Roosevelt organized his regiment of Rough Riders for the Spanish-American War. In 1899, the year McGinty joined the show, Cody added his simulated charge up San Juan Hill, which included veterans of Roosevelt's squad. By this time the show had 1,200 performers and Buffalo Bill was the most recognizable celebrity in the world.

The staging and rehearsals at Brooklyn's Ambrose Park began in 1894. The area in Sunset Park is now known as Bush Terminal.[3]

Looking down from Ambrose Park is a very pretty sight. One could see at a distance a dark speck in a great body of water where the East River and the Hudson River come together at the south point of New York City—the beginning of the bay that leads out to Sandy Hook. That is where all the ships arrive from the ocean beyond. The speck of darkness in that blanket of water is Governor Island, where many of the working people lived. A steamer service runs back and forth to the island every thirty minutes.

As we approached Ambrose Park, I could see the "big tops." There were rows and rows of the biggest tents that I had ever seen. Each tent was topped with a big mast that flew the American Flag. The park itself is on a flat and Buffalo Bill had built a number of log cabins back from the tents. They were built in 1894 when the show was smaller and were made of pine logs.

They looked just like some of the small towns that I had seen in the Rocky Mountains. The tall buildings in the cities on both sides made the place seem like it was hemmed in, and on a cloudy day a person felt like he was on a big flat with large canyons and mountains on either side.

The show held many interests for me the first few days and it was all very thrilling. I could hardly take time for my meals for wanting to look around and wonder what was in those tents. I especially wanted to see the fine horses that I knew the show had.

The first building that I saw much of was the dining hall and, even though I had lost all my appetite in the excitement, it was a wonder to me. It was large and roomy with long tables. All the meals were handled in a systematic manner. Each member of the show had a ticket that was punched for each meal. One waiter for every fifteen people served the tables and you could order whatever you wanted to eat. While [we were] with the show, our meals, transportation and bed were furnished as part of the contract. In all business matters the show was run to near-perfection.

After gulping down a few bites, I was out of the eating joint and ready to look around. One of the boys told me that they had several strings of pure white horses and that some of them were for the Rough Rider act. I found the horse tent right away and, sure enough, saw some of the prettiest horses that a man ever laid his eyes on. They must have had quite a job just finding that many white horses for the show. I was interested in all the horses and spent a long time visiting all the tents and the many fine animals, but that bunch of white horses sure held my attention and I often just sat in wonder at such a string of fine animals. I remembered when I was a kid and we all thought it was a good luck token to clap our hands every time we saw a white horse. The kids there could have spent a lot of time just clapping for white horses. I learned that the white horses were for the Rough Riders, the Sixth Cavalry, and the Cowboy Band.

I was sure tickled when I found out that I was to get to ride one of them in the show.

It took a lot of time and work to go over each act. We began with the overture, the "Star Spangled Banner" by the cowboy band under the direction of William Sweeney. Then came the Grand Review, introducing the Rough Riders of the World, then each individual act, beginning with Annie Oakley right on through the end of the show.

We rehearsed at Ambrose Park until late March. I had a part in several acts like all the other boys. I rode in the grand parade as the color bearer for the Rough Riders. I also rode in the act of the battle of San Juan Hill and was given the part of General Joe Wheeler in that act.

Buffalo Bill added the re-enactment of the Battle of San Juan Hill for the 1899 season and it drew the greatest applause of all every time we played. It featured two scenes, and for rehearsal we had a small replica of San Juan Hill built at Ambrose Park. The hill was not as complete as the one we had when we opened at Madison Square Garden in New York City a little later.

This act included a detachment of Roosevelt's Rough Riders, the Twenty-fourth Infantry, the Ninth and Tenth Cavalry, Grimes Battery, Garcia's Cuban Scouts, and several pack trains. The scene opened during the halt along the road to San Juan Hill and was called "The "Bivouac." The second scene, which was supposed to come after an elapse of a few hours, was called "Storming the Hill."

A Spanish blockhouse was placed on top of the replica hill and we were below the hill with artillery stationed behind us. As the scene opened everything was darkened except for the lights that gleamed from the soldiers' campfires. The soldiers were fully equipped and there were ambulance wagons, stretcher-bearers, and all.

The lights lowly came on as day broke on the morning of the charge up San Juan Hill. As the dawn burst into full glory, the band played the song "America." The Spaniards appeared at the top of the hill and started firing. We went up the hill and over the top, deployed in military fighting positions, taking cover and firing at the enemy as we went. Artillery shells burst over our heads and leading the field were those of us who played the parts of General Joe Wheeler, Colonel Wood, and Colonel Roosevelt.

As we neared the top of the hill and stormed the blockhouse, the Spaniards retreated. The Rough Riders pulled down the Spanish flag and hoisted "Old Glory" to the top as the band broke into the "Star Spangled Banner." Then, as the artillery moved off the field the band played the tune that had become the theme song of the Rough Riders: "There'll Be a Hot Time in the Old Town Tonight."

After the San Juan Hill act, the show rehearsed an act with the Arab riders. These were expert horsemen who had a distinct type of their own riding. Next came Johnny Baker's act. He was billed as "the world champion rifle shot." His performance was as colorful as any in the show and included such feats as shooting out a burning match and breaking small clay objects thrown in the air.

Each act was rehearsed as if the show played to an audience and the last part of the rehearsal covered more real-life action by Buffalo Bill. He gave an exhibition with the rifle and six-shooter, followed by a buffalo hunt that included a small herd of buffalo exhibited as the only remaining native herd of buffalo. Finally, at the end came a salute by the entire cast, which was similar to the "Grand Review" that opened the show.

As you can imagine, it took a lot of work to put on a show of this magnitude. A man named Nate Salsbury directed it and he was the best in the business. It was through his work that the show went over because he made us rehearse the acts until we had them down pat. The main object of the overall performance and organization of the show was to place the acts so that there is never a dull minute.

Actor-comedian Nate Salsbury joined the show as Cody's equal part-
ner and business manager in 1884, essentially saving the show since Cody
was at odds with his former partner and threatening to quit the business
altogether. Salsbury's shrewd sense of business and flair for staging are
credited with making Buffalo Bill's Wild West so successful.[4]

After many days of rehearsal we were ready for the annual
spring opening for the year 1899 at Madison Square Garden
in New York City. We moved into the Garden on March 26,
which that year happened to be on a Sunday. Our big opening
parade was supposed to be on Monday the 27th but it poured
down rain all that day. We postponed the parade to the following day, Tuesday, and opened for our first showing on
Wednesday night, March 29. We played to a packed house and
it was quite an experience for me, being my first night in Madison Square Garden.

On Friday, March 31, we played an afternoon performance
for the benefit of the orphanages and other institutions as well
as asylums around New York City. All together we played
thirty-one performances during our stay in the Garden and
each one drew a large crowd. Some of the time we played to
packed houses and the sign, "S.R.O." was hung on the box
office window. That was the first time I had ever seen such a sign
and when I asked them what it meant they told me that it was
"Standing Room Only." This abbreviation was an actor's real
enjoyment because it meant the show was a success. That season, I was told, proved to be one of the best that the show had
in its many years at New York's Madison Square Garden.

The 1899 performance at Madison Square Garden ran until April 15.
The New York Times reported that crowds "thronged" to the Garden.
On opening night, one of the featured guests included Major General Nel-
son Miles, famed Indian fighter and the top American army commander
at the time of the Spanish-American War. Miles had led the forces that
captured Puerto Rico.[5]

Buffalo Bill first started out with a small outdoor performance in Nebraska. It was a road show, traveling across country playing in several states and ending with a five-week stand at Coney Island, New York. Coney Island was a sort of carnival in itself and the Wild West show got a fine reception there and continued the following year. Coney Island is where the first horse race was run at night under lights.

In 1884 the show opened in the East and after touring Canada it headed down the Mississippi River by boat, playing the different towns on the way to New Orleans. At Rodney, Mississippi, the boat was wrecked in a bad storm, and all the show property was lost with the exception of the horses. That was in October, and Buffalo Bill, not to be outdone as the showman he was, had everything completely rebuilt and by Christmas week he opened in New Orleans.

During early 1885, the show worked other nearby southern states and finally closed the season at St. Louis, Missouri. The following season another mishap occurred that was a serious setback. It started when some sort of lung trouble affected the buffalo herd and sixteen of the prize animals died at the Garden in New York City.

On April 1, 1887, the show sailed for London, England, on the ship *The State of Nebraska*. It played a six-month engagement in London, and then went on to Manchester for another six months. After that it returned to the states and opened an engagement at Staten Island.

The scale of Cody's undertaking amazed the press on both shores of the Atlantic. When the show's company boarded the State of Nebraska *steamship for London, its entourage included "83 salon passengers, 38 steerage passengers, 97 Indians, 180 horses, 18 buffalo, 10 elk, 5 Texan steers, 4 donkeys, and 2 deer."[6]*

In 1889–90, the show sailed to Havre, France, on the ship *Persian Monarch*. It played a six-month engagement at Paris, then traveled for several other short engagements in France as well as Spain, Italy, Germany, and Austria. In October of 1890, part of the troupe returned to the United States while the remainder played the following season through Germany, Belgium, England and Scotland. They returned in 1892 to New York City at the close of the season and then played throughout the United States and gathered new and better acts as it continued, finally booking with Barnum and Bailey to complete an extremely large show and carnival.

During my first year with the show, we traveled a distance of eleven thousand miles in our many different daily routings. The show used the tracks of forty different railroads; was on the road for 200 days, and in that time gave 341 performances.

This was a typical performance schedule for Buffalo Bill's Wild West show in its heyday. About 135 towns were covered in twenty-four different states. The show's size required eleven acres of ground, and the "big top" alone covered 201,000 square feet.[7]

Show business was really interesting to me and my first year was especially thrilling. The work of setting up and tearing down, with all the people, cars, and equipment was really something to remember. There were 529 people employed in the different departments that were made up of nearly every nationality and trade. The group was large enough to make a small town itself. The show stables contained 325 horses and the baggage stock had 199 more. I could have said two hundred but who would want to tell a lie for one horse.

For transportation the show used thirty-four baggage wagons, two bandwagons, two water wagons, and two for lights, along with four buggies, two field [artillery] pieces with caissons and a Gatling gun. The show also carried eighty lengths of blue seats and eleven sections of reserved seats, giving seating room for more than thirteen thousand people.

There were twenty-four men who took care of the bronco stables, including two men who worked as blacksmiths. Sixty-three men were employed in the canvas department that took care of setting up and tearing down the big tops. On top of this, there were many different departments to give you an idea how much managing and efficiency was required to put a show on. There were the Wardrobe and Property Department, the Ammunition and Baggage Stock Department, as well as eight-horse drivers, six-horse drivers, four-horse drivers, and men who handled the pull-up teams. There was also a Blacksmith and Repair Department, plus Railroad, Side-Show, Canvas, and Confectionary Departments.

The show had a Cowboy Band, a Concert Company, and a Concert Orchestra, along with an official program publisher, electricians, firemen, lighting men, a Chandelier Department, jack setters, toe-pin drivers, blockers, and even someone in charge of kids.

There was the Big Top Stake and Chain Department, people in charge of dressing rooms, along with curtain men, front-door men, sail-makers, and cooks. The cook tent had a waiter, a helper, and a coffee boy for each of twelve tables that served various groups ranging from Indians to grooms and drivers to soldiers. There were also the dessert boys, dishwashers, and laundry men.

Looking back some forty years at that first opening night at Madison Square garden in 1899, it was really a big affair. The Garden is a lot different today, but even then it was an enormous place. The boxes held six people. The choice seats, of course, were the lower seats, and it was in one of those that Governor Theodore Roosevelt sat when he visited the show that year, and I felt especially proud that night when I learned he was in the box seats.

He seemed to like the cowboy acts the best and got a big kick out of the rifle shooting. I remember very well the first night he attended. He intently followed the riding of the bucking broncs, and after I had finished one that was a bit frisky he rose up in his seat and shouted "Bully." I heard the shout above the noise and recognized his voice and those familiar words.

In bronc riding—and I have a few cuts to show that I have spent some time at that business—you may have heard the term "sunfishing" or some other description of a horse's bucking movement. In my experience, the "crawdad" buck is the hardest to ride. While a "sunfisher" goes up and tries to dislodge the rider by twisting in the air and arching its back, a rider can use his legs on either side to balance and hold on, and if the horse goes down he can just step out of the stirrup and off. The "crawdad" bucker is especially difficult to handle if you're not used to him. When he goes up and comes down, he rears back and makes a "crawdad" action that upsets lots of riders over his head. Our shows had several animals that could really buck that way.

Before the show opened the first night, I went out into the arena to look around. I walked way up into the high seats, looked down, and wandered all over the building. The floor of the arena was covered with a thick coating of sawdust and in the middle, spelled out in big letters with sawdust, were the words, "Buffalo Bill's Wild West Show." Built in the northeast corner of the arena was San Juan Hill, which was hidden by a curtain. In the southeast corner there was a runway that led up from the basement where we entered. A curtain also hid the opening of this runway.

The show started at 8:30 that night and I was all ajitter. We were lined up behind the entrance curtain waiting for the cue. The band, located on a special stand at the west part of the arena, was also waiting and when they started playing "The Star Spangled Banner" the show was on.

When the curtain pulled back, the "Rough Riders of the World" rode out. We went directly to the reserved seat section and made a line, and behind us, all the other mounted riders in the troop formed lines. There were the Indians and cowboys, the Mexicans, Cossacks, Gauchos, and Arabs, along with the scouts, guides, and soldiers of the world, as well as the foreign and United States Army divisions. Then up in front of us rode

Annie Oakley and Johnny Baker, and, finally, to the front of the entire rank rode Buffalo Bill.

He raised his hat to the crowd in salute and his horse "Old Duke," a fine big red sorrel with a long mane and tail and white stocking feet, dipped his head and scraped his feet in a sort of bow, each time moving a step back. This made a grand sight the way Buffalo Bill was all decked out. He was a big man and so was his horse, which made it even more imposing.

After Buffalo Bill announced the show, introducing it as the Rough Riders of the World, Johnny Baker led the first line out, and as line after line formed an arc, the entire company was soon in one large circle. Johnny Baker then reversed the direction of the moving circle and rode out of the arena into the basement. This move was called the "mystic maze." It was performed at high riding speed and was very dangerous because the timing must be right. It was confusing to watch because the circle continued to get smaller and smaller and it was hard to tell just where a rider left the stage and got away from the circle. During all of this, Buffalo Bill's horse was backing and bowing until it reached the center of the arena at the same time the last person in the circle rode off. Buffalo Bill then turned and rode off amid loud applause.

This "Grand Review" made a spectacular sight with the multi-colored uniforms and costumes from all the countries. Each group of riders had their own flag and Jim Gabriel carried the cowboys'. It had a blue and white background with a buffalo on it. During the review I rode with the Rough Riders and carried the troop flag. Each nation had its own flag, but the American Flag led all of them.

The first act of the show, as I mentioned, was Miss Annie Oakley. Not long ago Hollywood produced a movie of her life. It was a great show but left out many characteristics of Annie Oakley that only one who had worked with her would have noticed. In the first place, Annie Oakley was beyond doubt the best rifle shot in the world. There was no hocus-pocus to her act. It was all very real and she had a very pleasant appearance, being small and attractive.

From the box seats she looked like a little girl because she wore short skirts and a large cowboy hat, giving her the appearance of even being smaller than she was. Short skirts were uncommon in those days because women's dresses often swept the ground. When Annie Oakley played with the show in Europe many of the royal families from different countries sent their men to the show to ask if they might invite the "little girl rifle shot" to dinner. Europe went wild over her act and her personality. During her act she had a little quirk involving the quick kick of her foot, and I have never seen it duplicated. It was very distinctive and had a way of moving her along with a snappy action and always brought a big hand from the audience. She was what I would call good-looking and had a smile for everyone. At the time I knew her she was past thirty but didn't look a day over twenty.

A few years later, Annie, who was naturally dark-haired, suddenly became white-haired. She had gone to Hot Springs, Arkansas. I do not remember exactly what happened there, but it had to do with leaving her in the steam bath too long.

Annie Oakley, a stage name she selected for herself, was really Phoebe Ann (Moses) Butler, who joined the show with husband Frank Butler in 1885. Dubbed "Little Sure Shot" by Chief Sitting Bull, she astonished crowds with her trick shooting for many years. The first movie about Annie Oakley, starring Barbara Stanwyck, was released in 1935. The Broadway production and movie Annie Get Your Gun *opened in 1946 with Ethel Merman in the title role, and a 1950 film starred Betty Hutton. Gail Davis played the part in a television series that started in 1954.*

The reference to "white hair" concerned an incident occurring in 1901 when an attendant at Hot Springs, Arkansas, left her in a steam bath for forty minutes instead of the usual sixty seconds. It scalded most of her skin and her hair turned white from the experience. Although she never returned to the show, she did perform some exhibition shooting with her husband through the early 1920s.[8]

During the years I worked for the show, Annie Oakley was married to Frank Butler. He always looked after the loading of her shells and took care of the guns and rifles. Frank had also been a good rifle shot. Several years before I joined the show, he was touring the country as an exhibition shooter. He was exceptionally good and thought he was the worlds' best, although he was not a braggart at heart.

Frank first met Annie (then known by her given name Phoebe) in Cincinnati, Ohio, in 1881 when a contest between them was set up. Frank thought he was a cinch for beating her even at shooting, but she beat him that day. They were married the following year and toured together for a while before joining Buffalo Bill's Wild West show in 1885. After that, he worked in support of her act and took care of the loading of her shells so that she'd have no accident.

Each act in the show was announced with great ballyhoo with the band blaring an added introduction. Following Annie Oakley was an act called the "Race of Races." It included horses from all over the world ridden by men of different nationalities, including American cowboys, Cossacks, Arabs, and Gauchos. They lined up in front of the reserved seats and raced around the arena for three laps. The winner of the race often varied, for the horses were well matched. The races were fixed, so the American horses got the majority of wins over the entire season.

The U.S. Artillery drill always got a big hand. These veterans of Captain Thorpe's Battery D of the Fifth Regiment came out in the arena with the big field guns and then paraded around before setting up. They lined up the field pieces toward the curtain that hid San Juan Hill and demonstrated setting up, firing, and taking the guns down. It was all done at top speed and was well drilled, but sometimes in the rush one of the heavy field pieces would topple over and off the carriages. Men were sometimes injured, being pinned beneath the heavy guns when this happened.

Battery D's members included drivers J. R. Meyerly, Thomas Gibney, Charles Wolff, Harry Wilkes, R. I. Clapman, and James Tyan. The sergeant was Herman Kanstein, and the other members were L. Wagner, R. Hegeman, C. Hobert, James Degnen, C. Trinagel, Pony Moore, and George Davis.

George Washington "Pony" Moore, was a former circus man, minstrel-show end man, and theatre manager, who, in the late 1880s and early 1890s, teamed with the famed "Bat" Masterson in promoting championship prizefights.[9]

There was also a drill by the Sixth United States Cavalry, veterans from Colonel Sumner's celebrated regiment from Fort Meyer, Virginia. These men wore the uniform the United States Army designed for the frontier. They rode western range horses, which were used in this manner for the first time.

At each performance in the Garden we expected special guests, who often stayed to eat with us. They included everyone from the president, to governors, senators, and statesmen, as well as society people and prizefighters. That was how I met many celebrities in those days and among them was prizefighter Bob Fitzsimmons. He always had a smile and a good word for all the boys and was very friendly and well liked by all of us.

During the time I was with the show the acts changed a little each year, but I remember those during my first year with the show best of all. In one of the acts called "A Prairie Emigrant Wagon Train Crossing the Plains," a wagon loaded with early-day pioneers entered the arena and stopped in front of the reserved seats. There, the people unhitched the team and went about making camp. After getting their pots and pans out and building a fire, a band of Indians rode up shooting and yelling as they formed a circle and rode around the wagon train. Suddenly, just in the nick of time, so it seemed, out rode Buffalo Bill and his men, who escorted the wagon train away to safety. The cowboys and scouts who rode with Buffalo Bill were Joe Esquivel, chief of the cowboys, along with John Franz, Silas Compton, Bert Schenck, Jim Gabriel, James Jennings, Walter Scott, Jack Joyce, Jesse Nelson, Tom Hunter, Bob Singletree, Lem Hunter, Carl Sorensen, A. M. McCann, and me.

Joe Esquivel, billed as "Chief of the Cowboys," performed with the show for many years. Once a working Mexican vaquero, he was born Antonio Esquivel.[10]

The Indians in the show included several real-life chiefs like Chief Iron Tail, Chief Black Fox, Chief Growler, Chief Iron Cloud, and Chief Has No Horse. There were also real-life Indian squaws named Mary Kills Enemy, Jennie Spotted Horse, and White Cow, and even one papoose named Willie White Bird. The Indian braves included Spotted Weasel, Good Horse, Comes Out Holy, Flying Horse, Standing Soldier, White Bird, Little Bull, Come Last, White Bonnet, Holy Bear, Eagle Fox, Pluck Porcupine, Red Calf, Jacob Iron Tail, and Charging Thunder. The interpreter for the group was David Bull Bear.

Lieutenant Standing Soldier, an Indian policeman, and Albert Has No Horse were Lakota Sioux, recruited for the show by Cody from the Pine Ridge Indian Reservation in South Dakota. Over the years Cody visited several reservations to recruit Indians for his show.[11]

When the Indian act came on, the arena was clear. The curtains hid everything. Suddenly the curtains opened and the Indians raced out into the arena and circled around giving the war whoop. This took the audience by surprise. It was thrilling and colorful with all the Indian costumes. Clad in breechcloths with war bonnets and leggings hung with bells, riding their paint ponies without saddles, [they] took the audience back to the Wild West.

After the braves came the squaws; some walked carrying papooses strapped to their backs on boards with rawhide thongs. Others rode with poles from pony to pony, and between the poles were baskets made from sticks and rawhide. Some of the larger Indian children were riding in these baskets. When they had all reached the center of the arena, they started their dances. As the drums beat, the chants began and in this ceremonial display it seemed that each Indian tried to outdo the other.

One of the Indian boys, who was an excellent dancer, died on my second year with the circuit. I recall that he got into a pecan grove and ate some green pecans, which the doctor gave as the cause for his death. It was a real loss to the act and was noticed more by the show's performers than the audiences.

Following the Indians came the gymkhana race. The gymkhana race was a clown race in which the cowboys were dressed in the regular clothes, but clowned around in a special riding act. They made a dash on their horses halfway around the arena, then they got off, took off their coats, turned them inside-out, put them back on again, rolled a cigarette, lit it, and then got back on their horses and finished the race.

Gymkhana *is a term of Hindu origin brought into the language by the British, meaning an event held to test the skills of competitors such as in athletic contests or equestrian meets.*[12]

The show's Pony Express act was also taken from Buffalo Bill's experiences. As a young man, he had carried the mail on the route to Fort Hays, Kansas. Buffalo Bill had been swift afoot as well as on horseback so it was natural that a top rider be used for this. The man chosen was Jack Joyce, who didn't have an equal when it came to straight riding because he was fast as forked lightning with a horse.

To stage this act the arena was set up with several mail stations that were supposed to be along his route. When it opened,

Jack came out with a mail sack on his saddlehorn, riding just as fast as he could. He circled the arena and about halfway around was the first "station" where a man waited with another mail sack and a fresh horse. As he reached this station he would slow up a bit, grab the saddlehorn of the fresh mount, then leap into the air from one saddle to another and ride off as fast as the wind to another station. Jack also cut up some while he was riding, like swinging from one side of the horse to the other, which made quite a show for the audience.

Pennsylvania-born Jack Joyce spent ten years with the show, starting in 1898. The top-notch bronc rider also performed in the roping and riding act staged by comedian Will Rogers in a New York theatre. After leaving Buffalo Bill's Wild West show, Joyce toured Europe as a bronc buster and trick rider for a circus before establishing his own circus in Denmark about 1910.[13]

Another great show act was Johnny Baker's shooting. Johnny first met Buffalo Bill in South Platt [*sic*], Nebraska, when he was just a youngster, and his hero worship of Bill got him into show business. At first Johnny helped out by holding Bill's horse, blacking his boots and running errands, but Bill took such a liking to him that he adopted him as a foster son and began teaching him all the tricks of riding and shooting. Johnny was such a good pupil that he soon had mastered the technique of the six-gun and rifle as well as riding. [On the arena floor] he could shoot while standing on his head and over his shoulder backwards using a mirror. Sometimes he took over Buffalo Bill's shooting act, breaking small clay balls in the air while riding at full speed.

When he died, Buffalo Bill was buried on Lookout Mountain near Denver, and it was Johnny who helped build a memorial for him there that later became a museum. Many of Buffalo Bill's belongings, given to him by royalty all around the world, wound up in the museum. After Johnny Baker died in later years, his wife contributed most of his possessions to the museum.

Baker was only six years old in 1876 when he first met Cody and became known as "Buffalo Bill's boy." Lew Baker, Johnny's father, was a former stagecoach way station operator in western Nebraska and had recently moved to North Platte. The term "Bill's boy" was informal as Johnny still lived with his own family, but constantly begged Cody to let him join the show. With his parents' permission, Johnny finally joined, and under Cody's tutelage he won a national marksman championship by the time he was fourteen. Baker went on to serve with the show for thirty-three years, performing over 12,600 shooting exhibitions during his tenure. A crack shot with both a pistol and a rifle, Baker could hit targets while standing on his head and specialized at shooting objects thrown into the air. At a show in Hamburg, Germany, he broke one thousand flying objects out of 1,016 shots fired. Baker also served as director of entertainment or stage manager for the show.

Buffalo Bill died in Denver on January 10, 1917. Shortly before his death he remarked to family members that he wanted to be buried on nearby Lookout Mountain near Golden, Colorado, a picturesque location with a view of the plains and Rocky Mountains. Johnny Baker carried on with the show through November of 1917, at which time the final curtain fell on Buffalo Bill's Wild West. In 1921, Baker started the Buffalo Bill Memorial Museum at the Lookout Mountain location, personally overseeing its operation until his death in 1931.

Johnny's first wife was Jule Keen, the daughter of the Wild West Show's treasurer. She died after the birth of their second daughter, and in 1900 Johnny married Miss Olive Burgess of Holyoke, Massachusetts.[14]

Mrs. [Olive] Baker was a real nice person who treated us all well. She was a serious person, however, and joked around very little, unlike some of us who got a big kick out of a joke or trick. I had known her but a short time when I sort of got in over my head kidding around with her. One year, when there was a New York law that required the show to close on Sundays, a bunch

Billy behind the curtains at a Buffalo Bill outdoor show in 1900. Glenn D. Shirley Western Americana Collection, National Cowboy & Western Heritage Museum.

of us boys went down to Coney Island on a sightseeing trip. While I was moseying around, I ran across Johnny's wife and, as small talk would go, she asked me what I was doing there. I told her that I had been looking around and had got all mixed up and was lost.

I was just kidding her, but she took me seriously and was very concerned. She took my hand and walked me to the train, and after showing me which one to take back she carefully gave me directions to the hotel. She was very serious and tried to make everything very plain so I could understand.

By this time I was in too deep to back out, so I let her walk me right up to the car I was supposed to get on to go back to the city. I said "goodbye," walked onto the train car, and then walked right out the other side when she wasn't looking. I had to avoid running into her the rest of that day.

Getting back to the show, another of the acts I was involved in was called "Cowboy Fun." It was billed as "eighteen minutes of thrills and spills" and it started with Buffalo Bill leading us into the arena. Some wild horses had been turned loose just a few seconds before, and we immediately took out after them with our ropes. We missed sometimes, but Buffalo Bill hardly ever missed "Old Paint" on the first go around. After catching these horses, the cowboys rode them, and in most of the shows I was picked to ride the first horse. For this particular act the show had a horse named "Jubilee." It was one of the worst buckers that I ever ran across, even though they had several that were plenty mean.

Now I know that in some shows the riding acts are staged and the animals used are trained to buck, but that was not the case here. Each of those horses was really wild and mean and the riders were chosen for their ability to handle such broncs. I guess that was what made Buffalo Bill's shows such a success, because it was the real stuff, no bunk or fake about it.

Other features of this act involved picking up handkerchiefs and trick roping on horseback. The cowboys, including me, rode into the arena at a snappy pace, then reached down from the saddle and picked up white handkerchiefs that lay on the ground. All this brought a big hand from the crowd, and even today trick roping and bucking broncs draw huge crowds at rodeo events all over the world.

CHAPTER 6

Cowboys, Characters, and Show Shenanigans

DURING the years that I was bucking horses in the show, I was the first one up to ride most of the time. I don't know why they picked me; I guess they just wanted to see me get throwed, which I did several times. But I didn't mind so much getting throwed; it was where and when I lit that I didn't like. It was all a very thrilling time because no one ever knew just what was going to happen, not even the riders. Every bronc rider stands a good chance of getting throwed. They never get so good that it doesn't happen once in a while. If they get careless and start showing off, they usually find themselves without a saddle under them and bite the dirt.

The broncs get plenty smart too, and if you don't believe this, you should have seen some of the moves these horses made when they start bucking. The horses with Buffalo Bill's show were the meanest anywhere, and they showed us all plenty of action, but there never was a horse that could not be rode, and there never was a rider that could not be throwed.

While with Buffalo Bill, there were folks who would bring in broncs that he figured were too tough for the riders in the show. They, too, had the idea that the show animals were trained. Now we rode these horses for them, but Buffalo Bill never allowed them to be ridden during a performance, first because they might get out there and not buck at all, and second because many of them were poor and not too well fed and did not come up to the standard of the fat broncs of the show.

Another one of the boys in our cowboy act was Walter Scott, also known as Death Valley Scotty. He really had class when he was with the show, for he not only was an excellent rider, but in his dress and his action he was almost a show by himself. His hats were special made for him by a big hat company in Philadelphia. They had an extra high crown with a sharp peak and the brims were not quite as wide as the common hat of this style. He designed the hats himself.

Back then, Scotty was not as heavy as he became in later years, but was a good-sized fellow with a broad face that lit up like the sun after a storm when he smiled. He was a real partner too, and in for most anything. He was heavily muscled and a tough-hardened westerner, the picture of a real cowboy. With his white angora chaps, his flashy shined boots, saddle stirrups with tapaderas that hung about a foot below the stirrup, and a highly decorated saddle that he called a "California Center-Fired," he really was a sight when he rode out into the arena. He was a crowd favorite and always got a big hand because he typified what people pictured as a real westerner.

One of the last riders of the bucking horses was a man by the name of Bert Schenck. Bert was what I would call a great bronc rider. He put the finishing touch to the riding act by raking some of the mean ones all over the arena and letting them buck to their heart's content. Bert was probably one of the greatest riders that I have ever known. He also worked with the Major Cummins' Wild West Shows at St. Louis during the World's Fair. He later went to the Philippines, where he was on the police force at Manila.

Frederick T. Cummins's Wild West Show performed along the "Pike," the amusement attraction area, at the St. Louis World's Fair in 1904. His own "Congress of Rough Riders" performed riding and roping tricks and staged a series of frontier battles along with several famous Indians, including Chief Joseph and American Horse.[1]

The Mexican roping act was also quite a show in itself. The sergeant of the Mexican ropers was Vincente Oropeza, who could rope any combination of a horse's feet and even rope the tail or body with the rider and all. He was also the originator of the rope-twirling act, which is where Will Rogers got the idea for twirling a rope. Oropeza had a real knack for rope spinning and he was just as good at it whether on horseback or afoot.

Will would sometimes come over and stay with our show for days at a time. I remember once in Philadelphia, Will watched Vincente Oropeza spin the ropes and do his tricks with the loop. Will Rogers had added several touches to his own rope-twirling act by then. He could twirl the lariat with both hands and keep up a line of chatter all at the same time. I've seen many trick ropers in my time, but I've never seen one who could work the rope from as many places about his body as Will Rogers could, and all the time be making a good speech.

Will Rogers grew up with a rope in his hand, working on his father's ranch in Indian Territory. At the 1893 World's Fair in Chicago, teenager Rogers saw a performance by trick roper Vincente Oropeza, the undisputed master of the lariat. Rogers immediately set out to become the world's "poet lariat" and spent endless hours practicing, perfecting, and trying new tricks.[2]

Vincente Oropeza was a bullfighter, too, and he once told me some of the tricks of that trade. He said that when a bull charged, the bull would close his eyes within about thirty feet of you and then continue in a straight line after that. A good bullfighter would sidestep after the bull closed his eyes and never get caught. He also told me that bulls, as well as cows, were color-blind and would get infuriated at any bright color. Oropeza said that red was used in bullfighting because it was a blood sport.

One of Will Rogers's closest friends with the show was Tom Isbell. Tom had been raised near Will's home in Oklahoma and was a fellow Rough Rider who served with me in Cuba. Some of the other cowboys in our act included Silas Compton, our cowboy chief. He was a great rider and had been in show business and riding exhibitions before signing up with Buffalo Bill. After leaving Bill's show, he went with the Ringling Brothers Circus.

Another great rider was Jim Jennings, who performed in exhibition matches all over the world, winning a good many of them, too. Then there was R. P. Mason, whom we all called "Bronco Pete." R. P. married a trapeze artist while the show was playing at the Olympia Hall in London, England, one of the largest in the world at that time. He finally took up trapeze work himself and, after returning to the United States, became quite an artist at it.

Another one of the better riders of the show was Lem Hunter. He married Blanche McKenny, who had a show of her own in which she was billed as the woman rider of the world's highest jumping horses. They were married while Lem was with the Buffalo Bill shows and afterwards they started a show of their own called the "Blanche McKenny and Hunter Racing Combination." They used Roman chariots and standing racing combinations in their act. Blanche was a top-notch rider and a good horse trainer.

During this period I got to know Will Rogers and admired him much for his showmanship and knack for handling the rope. [Later,] many people thought of him as only a trick roper and twirler because of his stage and screen appearances, but he was also a good roper on a horse as well as a good tie-down cowboy.

Roping has changed considerably in the rodeos and on the range. Horses are taught different ways of holding a calf or steer while the riders tie them. In those days, after the cowboy caught the calf, the horse turned its back to the steer and held the slack on the animal. Nowadays, most of the horses have their heads towards the steer when the cowboy ties them.

A short time before the World's Fair, Buffalo Bill's show played St. Louis and staged a big rodeo contest at the fairgrounds. "Booger" Red from San Angelo, Texas, furnished the

broncs for the riding contests. They were picked from all over
the country.

*Samuel Thomas "Red" Privett got the name "Booger" because some
firecrackers unexpectedly blew up and disfigured his face, after which people said the accident "sure did 'booger' him up." Born in 1864 in Erath
County, Texas, he went into bronc busting when there was no time limit
to the ride. Red had a small Wild West show that traveled by wagon route
and played in little towns where he challenged local riders with some of
his best wild broncs. At age sixty-one he came out of retirement and rode
a bucking horse for exhibition at Fort Worth. He died two weeks later.*[3]

Riders and ropers gathered from all over the United States to
take part and Will Rogers had his horse shipped in from Claremore, Oklahoma, for the contest. His mother came along, too,
because she was afraid Will might get hurt, as he was a bit reck-
less in his roping. Will liked to rope the biggest ones and she
knew it.

The horse Will used for roping was a small dun that weighed
about 800 pounds. He was a fast pony in those days. Buffalo
Bill allowed one rider and one roper from his show to enter the
contests, too. Vincente Oropeza entered in the roping contest
that year and while he was good at roping, he was a bit slow at
tying. Will Rogers made the best time overall and pulled down
the 750-dollar prize. A short time before this, I had broken my
shoulder and I had to watch the bucking contests from the side-
lines. A man by the name of California Jack won it and Jack
Joyce got second. Jack was the man we entered from Buffalo
Bill's show.

While we were playing at the Garden, a bunch of us roomed
across the street at a place called the Putman House. One season while we were there, Will Rogers was doing his vaudeville
act at Hammerstein's Paradise Roof Theatre, which was about
five blocks up the street. After the show a bunch of the boys
would come down to the Putman House and sit around visit-

ing with each other. Scotty [Walter Scott] and Rogers were great kidders and were always pulling gags. I liked to sit around just listening to them go after each other and different members of the troupe. At the time, none of us really thought of them or the others becoming very famous for we were all just show boys together.

The Hammerstein was the first big stage appearance for Will Rogers except the part he had with the Mulhall Wild West Show that played at Madison Square Garden. One year when they were moving into the Garden, a big steer broke loose. Will took his rope and made quick work of roping and tying that steer down in front of a big crowd that looked on. This showed everyone that he was a good cowboy as well as vaudeville star, and it got quite a big play up in the New York papers, especially the *New York Herald*.

The incident with the steer took place on April 27, 1905, when Rogers was working with Zack Mulhall's Wild West Show at Madison Square Garden. The steer reportedly defied cowboys and police by jumping a railing and climbing into the grandstand, causing patrons to flee in panic. Rogers roped and subdued the animal, eventually getting it back into the arena.

The Hammerstein Paradise Roof was one of the finest vaudeville stages in New York. Producer and stage manager William Hammerstein (father of Oscar Hammerstein II) later moved Rogers to his more spacious Victoria Theatre.[4]

During one of Will's first appearances at the Hammerstein, he was twirling his rope when he dropped it and it fell at his feet. Will's quick and ready wit came instantly into play and he remarked in his well-known drawl, "Well, I'd rather have it around my feet than around my neck." The simple statement brought down the house with roars and applause, and they never caught on that it was only an accident. Will then made the dropped rope a part of his act, which helped him in his start as a vaudeville actor when he was billed as the "cowboy humorist of the world."

Will told me that if some part of his act didn't seem to go over with the audience he'd try it for three more times. If it still didn't go over, then he threw it out of the routine. There is no doubt that Will Rogers knew how to play to an audience's reaction. The thing I remember about him the most, that really set him apart, was his ability to speak. He knew what to say and when to say it and this made for great entertainment.

Every time I met him he would ask me about some of the boys and how they were getting along and I would find out from him how some of the other boys were doing. He always seemed to know where everyone was and if it happened that someone had gotten into some sort of trouble, he would remark that they were just not doing too well.

Scotty [Walter Scott] was like that too. He could be as witty as anyone, but his wit was fast and his brain seemed to work like lightning. Will Rogers was slower in his answers and his wit seemed to carry a deeper meaning. Both were well liked by the boys and all the show folks, and as I sit and reminisce of those days, it seems that their companionship and friendship meant more to me than most anything I can remember. It would take a book to describe the life of either Death Valley Scotty or Will Rogers.

When Walter Scott left the Buffalo Bill show, he pulled out for Death Valley. He told us that he knew a spot where we could go out in the valley and pan out more gold with a horn spoon than we could make at the show the rest of our lives. I told him that I didn't want to go out there and starve to death.

Before he left the show he married a girl by the name of Lizzie [sic], who was a nurse at a hospital in Boston. He seemed to be crazy about her and always looked forward to the day he would get to see her, but that all changed, and in later years he tried to keep away from her because she sued him for a large sum of money. Sometimes Scotty had a large sum of money, but when Lizzie got after it, a fellow by the name of Johnson ended up owning everything and Scotty wound up broke.

Death Valley Scotty made and lost money several times during his colorful career. Scott married Ella Josephine Millius, sometimes called "Jack" by Scotty, in 1900. A self-promoter and con man, he bilked many investors with claims to bogus gold mines. One who turned Scotty's deception to his advantage was Chicago millionaire Albert Johnson. In the 1920s he partnered with Scotty to build the famous "Death Valley Castle" that became a popular hotel and tourist attraction. By the 1930s Scotty was estranged from his wife, and in 1936 she sued him for support, at which time it became known that Scotty was virtually penniless and that Johnson, his front man, owned everything. In 1970, the National Park Service purchased the "castle" and it became the most popular feature of Death Valley National Park.[5]

Scotty knew every trail in Death Valley after working there when he was young. Sometimes he would pack up his burros and be gone for a long period of time. No one ever knew where he went, and while many tried to follow, he managed to keep his whereabouts a secret. He pulled many tricks on those who sought to find his mines and always got a big kick out of a joke on the boys, and he pulled some good ones on folks that tried to follow him into the valley.

Sometimes he'd start out for a mine and, knowing that someone was following, he'd find a hiding place and then take pot shots at them with his long-range rifle, not shooting to hit them but to scare them back. He sometimes did this even when he was not going to one of his mines, just to make people afraid to follow him.

One time Scotty went into Barstow, California, to charter a train for a nonstop trip to Chicago. The agent thought he was crazy and sent him to Los Angeles, where he arranged for the train with Santa Fe railroad officials. His chartered train made a record fast trip east and was front-page news in newspapers all over. In Chicago, Scotty started seeing the town and spent a lot of money. He was a liberal spender and gave newsboys dollars instead of nickels for a paper.

This was a typical self-promotion scheme by Scotty. After boasting he could break the rail speed record from Los Angeles to Chicago, he obtained the backing of a Los Angeles mining engineer and, in 1905, he chartered a three-car train, the Coyote Special, *at a cost of $5,500. Arriving in Chicago in just forty-four hours and fifty-four minutes, his train broke the existing record for the 2,265-mile journey. "We got there so fast that nobody had time to sober up," was the way Scotty described the feat.*[6]

In my first year with the show, Buffalo Bill himself gave me the honor of making the first moving picture of a bucking horse. I was called into the main office one day right before the opening at Madison Square Garden and told to report to Ambrose Park.

When I arrived I found two men who were to take the pictures. I had never seen a motion picture camera before. It was a big square box covered with a black cloth. This was in the early days of the moving picture industry and the camera had to be set up stationary. The men had quite a time deciding how the picture should be made because they wanted to make sure that the horse didn't come toward them.

They set their camera to focus at a distance but after talking it over they couldn't seem to get together on this. What they really wanted was a close-up shot without any danger. They kept telling me that the camera costs so many hundreds of dollars, and that it must not be broken. But I had a feeling that they were just as much scared of the horse hurting them as the camera.

Finally, I figured out that the best thing to do was to have the horse headed toward the regular horse tents. Ambrose Park was winter quarters for the animals and the horses would probably head right for the tents. They finally decided to try this and they set up the camera as close as they dared. When they were ready, I got on the horse and the boys turned him loose. He made for the tents just as I figured he would but as we got close he hit a tent peg or something and went down. I jumped clear and was not hurt.

I felt bad because the horse had jumped only a few minutes. I went over to the men and told them I'd ride him again but they said that they had just what they wanted. They said that when the horse "upset" that was what they wanted to get. They got a good picture of it, so I am told, but I never got to see it. The movie was shown at the York and Keys Theatre at Thirteenth and Broadway. Some of the boys said they saw it and it was a good clear picture.

The cameraman told me that this was the first time a picture of a cowboy on a bucking horse was ever taken. It would probably seem pretty tame to people of today, who see cowboys on charging horses whose feet seem to run right over the camera.

During each season the Buffalo Bill and P. T. Barnum shows always played at the nation's capital. It was a thrill and honor for me to be near the White House and the center of government for whose principles I had fought in Cuba. We usually spent three days in Washington, D.C., and in 1900, President McKinley invited Buffalo Bill to come to the White House on Sunday. He was to bring two of the members of the show from each country represented. This was a great honor and we all waited, hoping that Buffalo Bill would choose one of us to go. I had no idea who he would choose outside of Johnny Baker, who was like a son to him.

The next morning Buffalo Bill picked out the men to go and I was fortunate enough to represent the United States and the Rough Riders. I rode carrying the flag at the head of column alongside Buffalo Bill and a representative of the cowboys. We were all dressed in the uniforms and regalia that represented the different countries and units of the show, and everyone rode white horses. This made quite an imposing sight. There were the Russians carrying their flag, the Germans in their uniform, the Filipinos, the Hawaiians, and on down the line with every country represented, as well as the Indians.

We arrived at the White House just before ten A.M. We rode up to the north side of the White House to a large porch. There was no one on the porch but in the doorway we could see a butler. He just stood there and we sat on our horses and waited for what seemed quite a while. After a time a man came up to him and said something and down he came to meet us. Buffalo Bill got off his horse and ordered us to get down so we tied our horses to each other's bridle and the butler held them all.

We marched in to a big waiting room and assembled our groups and flags together and then sat down and waited. We all just looked at each other. I've often wondered if those other fellows were as ill at ease as I was. I was glad to be up there but I was certainly scared and so was everyone else. If the butler hadn't come in soon, we probably would have left. He told us that the President would be in shortly.

When President McKinley came in, we made formal introductions. Buffalo Bill went around the room with him and we each rose and were introduced. After this, which took some time, President McKinley stepped to the center of the room and made a brief speech. I don't remember exactly what he said but I know each of us felt very proud of his compliments to our show. He presented Buffalo Bill with a white horse and Buffalo Bill in turn thanked him and expressed appreciation for the other members of the show for his kind invitation to the White House. We then rode back to the show grounds. I really felt proud to be picked to go because everyone in our bunch would have given nearly anything to go.

Buffalo Bill turned the white horse he got from President McKinley over to Lon Muxlow and as long as Lon was with the show he rode this horse. Lon was a good cowboy and a good rider. He was sure tickled to be riding the President's horse. Later Lon came back to Oklahoma and joined up with the police force in Guthrie. A few years ago he was shot by a man who was bootlegging whiskey into Indian Territory.

On the night of September 7, 1913, Guthrie police officers Lon Muxlow and Isaac Caldwell attempted to arrest a local man for bootlegging whiskey. As Muxlow tried to take him into custody, the suspect pulled a gun and mortally wounded both officers.[7]

Back in 1899, show business was pretty much like it is now. The idea was to attract attention and make the acts seem real. To do this, it took hours of practice, and new acts were added each year.

When we were in Chicago we tried a new style of cowboy act and it came near being a bad stunt. We played Chicago for several weeks and always had a large attendance at each performance. We also had many celebrities at those shows, and in those days many of the richer people of Chicago wore high hats and derbies. It sometimes looked more like opening night at the opera when the reserved seats filled, so we decided to stage an act from the reserved seat section. One of the cowboys in the bronco act was to dress up like a Chicago dude with coat, high-top silk hat, cane and all. Then he was to ride a bronco with these duds on.

When they picked out someone to do the act, they passed the buck to me. I didn't know just how it would work out, but I thought I would give it a whirl. I dressed in the fancy clothes, put on my high hat, and laid a gold-crowned cane across my arm. I couldn't roll the cane on my fingers though, like some of those dudes could.

When the cowboy act started, I was up in the reserved seat section. I had slipped in a short time before and was sitting there taking it all in. When they started riding the wild horses, I jumped up and pushed my way through the crowd and hollered that I wanted to show those would-be cowboys how to ride a bronco. The reserved seat section was full that night, as well as the rest of the arena. I figured there were about twenty thousand people there.

As I pushed down towards the arena floor, the folks in the seats kept telling me to go back and sit down. I just kept on going, begging them to let me ride and show up them cowboys. As I got near the arena railing, nearly everybody got up on their feet and hollered for me to go back. Several women and men grabbed me by the arms and tried to keep me from going down to the arena. This sure did attract attention because everyone thought here was a Chicago dude that was going to get killed.

I finally made my way into the ring and I got hold of a bronco and the boys held him while I got on. It must have made some sight, me crawling on that horse with my long-tail coat, my tall hat, and cane. I'd always been used to riding with spurs and when this horse started pitching and bucking I tried to grab his sides with my heels, but his sides felt as slick as if he had been greased. He was a real good bucker and pitched until I thought maybe I should have gone back when the audience told me to. I lost my hat, my gold-headed cane, and I nearly lost my seat. I really was lucky to stay astride that horse, and was plenty glad when I got down.

I got a big hand from the audience but that was the first and last trial of the addition to the new act. I told them right then and there that if they wanted to add that trick to the act they would have to get someone else besides me. It is a dangerous business in those kind of duds and I was really glad when they decided to change the act.

The Buffalo Bill show did not perform on Sunday. Not only was it a day of rest for the boys, it was our only time to see the town and its many sights. There was always someone from the city who would come out and take the boys around. These hosts were of the richer class who knew every crook and turn of the city and the boys who went on the excursions always saw and had the best of everything.

This was especially true for the Rough Riders in the show because the people were thrilled with winning the Cuban War, so we were well received everywhere. Many of us were invited to stay at the homes of some of these rich people and were given the time of our lives. We were also invited to parties and such after the show, even though it was a bit tiresome sometimes. We all wanted to attend these functions and learned always to be on time, for it was a bad error to show up late.

One man I remember especially was a diamond dealer in New York City named Charley Labaugh. He often traveled abroad bringing back diamonds for recutting and selling. He took a great interest in the Rough Riders. He was a personal friend of Teddy Roosevelt and was a great admirer of those who had been in the war. He would come on Sunday and pick up a bunch of us boys and take us all around town and pay all the bills. He was a good spender and showed us all a good time. Naturally, we liked him and he often came to the show and ate with us. He had a way of getting each man to tell his life history and especially tell him everything about the war and their work in the show. He remembered each man he met and could call him by name, just as if they were old friends.

One Sunday he took a bunch of us boys to Coney Island. It was a live bunch and he took us through nearly everything there. He asked us if we wanted to go through "Hell and Heaven" [a cycloramic sideshow] and most of us thought he was joking, until we entered one place at Coney which was a great scene and show. Later, we went down to the beach and sat in a section where some high board seats looked down on a pony ride. Now this pony ride was just a narrow lane between two big buildings which ran down to the beach, and the people were charged twenty-five cents to ride down and back. The boys sure got a kick out of seeing those folks trying to ride, for some of them really looked awkward getting on and trying to ride those ponies. They had a fellow there that helped the people get on; he was a big fellow, weighing about two hundred pounds. He would pick up some people and throw them up on the horse, Sometimes they were so scared they would hold their legs together and could hardly get astraddle the horses.

We got to laughing and cutting up and Charley asked me to go down and show them how to ride. I didn't want to go down there and ride those little knot-headed ponies, but they kept after me and Charley had been so good to all of us, so I decided to please him.

I stepped up to the big fellow and gave him the money for the ride. He looked at me kind of disgusted like when I told him I didn't know how to get on. Then he grabbed hold of me and threw me up on the pony. I held my legs together like I had seen some of the other people do, and fell off on the other side of the horse. I kept a hold of the horse's neck to keep from falling on my face. He came around and helped pick me up and then he tried it again. I just kept holding my legs together, making a grab and falling off each time.

He asked me if I was scared of the pony, and I told him that I did not think so for he hadn't done anything to me. After a few more times he gave up and gave me back my money and told me to get out. He said, "Who told you that you could ride any way?"

The boys up in the seats were just killing themselves laughing. They begged me to go back down there and show that big fellow I could ride. I told them no because the big fellow would kill me if he found out I was ribbing him. I just wanted to get away from there, for I was afraid he would catch on that the boys were laughing at him, so we finally left.

In my second year with the Buffalo Bill show, I rode a new bronc from the Crow Indian Reservation in Montana when we played Madison Square Garden. The show always had a good batch of new bucking horses added each year and these broncs were the "real McCoy." When Buffalo Bill advertised that the horses in the bronc riding contest were wild, that meant they were really wild.

The horse that I was to ride that night was a real high jumper. When he pitched, he really went up in the air. As soon as I mounted he went to work and after a short pitching run he made for the reserved seat section, still pitching and bucking. He went up in the air and as he came down he caught my leg around the banister on the box seats. He had to be plenty high in the air to hit that banister.

In the crush against the banister my leg was broken but I held on. I can see these folks in the box seats now. They were clearing out fast, thinking the horse was coming right over into the seat with them. They got out of that section plenty quick and I got the horse turned and rode him to the exit where I grabbed the curtain hanger and let him go.

As I swung off, with my leg hanging, the cold sweat broke out all over me. The boys helped me down and eased me until after the show was over. Then I was taken to the home of a doctor friend of mine by the name of Doctor [Harry] Thorpe. He was in attendance at the show that night and was also a staff doctor at Bellevue Hospital under Dr. Curtis. He called Dr. Curtis to his home and he came to set my leg.

I was sure treated swell at the Doctor's home and had many sympathetic visitors. Some very pretty girls from New York City called on me and I still have their cards. The night after I was hurt, three Mexicans were injured at the show. When I was hurt I tried not to let on, and I was informed later that people didn't know my leg was broken until the papers came out the next day.

The New York Times *reported that Billy's wild ride into the arena's box seat railing resulted in multiple injuries: "McGinty, one of the Roosevelt Rough Riders who was seriously injured on Monday night [April 30] by being thrown from a bucking pony against the side of the ring, had three ribs broken and two bones in one leg." The story also correctly predicted that he would be laid up for several weeks.*

Dr. Harry Thorpe, who treated Billy, was a New York physician who had served with the Rough Riders' medical staff in Cuba.[8]

I was in Dr. Thorpe's home for five weeks, and by that time the show had already moved on to Boston. Johnny Baker sent me twenty-five dollars for expense money and told me to go by the Bellevue Hospital and pick up one of the Mexicans who was able to travel at that time, and catch up with the show at Boston.

Now this Mexican could not speak our language very good, so he could not travel alone, and I was still on my crutches, and could hardly get around. Dr. Thorpe went down and got our tickets for the steamer on the Hudson. He checked my trunk to Boston and gave me the tickets.

At Albany we were to change from the boat to a train for our trip into Boston. After a short trip on the boat, we were called from our stateroom and asked for our tickets. I had them when we boarded, but I hunted and hunted and could not find them. The man told me to go back to our stateroom and look for them. I looked all over and still couldn't find them. He told me I would just have to pay our fare and asked me if I had any money. I told him that I did not have much but I guessed it was enough, but that I wasn't going to pay my fare twice.

The boat conductor told me that they would have to take us back to New York City then, but I argued a bit and asked him how I could have possibly checked my trunk without a ticket. He saw that the trunk was checked all right. I explained that I was due at the show in Boston as soon as possible but that didn't seem to get us anywhere. He told us to get on back to the stateroom and they were going to take us to New York City, but the boat waited until the train came in and shortly before that time they came in and told us we could board the train. He explained that we would have to get a ticket for the train ride anyway.

So we got on the train and after awhile here came the conductor and asked for our tickets. I gave him the trunk check. He said he didn't want my trunk check, he wanted our tickets. I told him that I had lost them. He bluntly told us to get off at the next station and get a ticket and away he went. I never said anything but I never got off and after awhile he came around and asked if I had my ticket yet. I told him that I had not and that I had bought one once and that I wasn't going to buy another. He started reading the riot act to me and I just sat there and didn't say much. He left in a little while and there was a fellow sitting close to me leaned over and said, "Listen, buddy, if I were you, I'd get off and get a ticket. This is Sunday and the laws are very strict on Sunday." I thanked him, but told him that the Mexican and I had purchased one ticket and that was enough.

Then the conductor came back again and he was plenty hardboiled. He started getting personal so I told him what I thought. I told him that my trunk check to Boston was good proof that I had bought tickets. He said that he didn't know but what someone else was riding on our tickets, but I let him know I didn't think so. I also told him that the only way that he could get the Mexican and me off the train was to pick us up and throw us off.

We finally got into Boston and I had a cab driver take my trunk to the show grounds. I tried to think what became of those tickets, and the only way I know they could have possibly gotten away was when we first boarded the boat. I had gone out on deck to look at the Hudson River and I pulled my handkerchief from my pocket. It was windy that day and they could have blown overboard. I figured that was the only chance I could have lost them.

Six weeks after my leg was broken, I was riding broncs again. At first I would take about eighteen feet of rubber bandage and wrap my leg up real tight. Right after the act, I would remove the bandage. In a short time my leg was solid as ever.

Many outstanding things happened during our show trips across the country. I often received requests for favors and some of them were most odd. A special one that I recall came from a friend of mine in Washington, D.C., who was in the Department of War. He followed the route of our show and one day shortly before we reached Cleveland, Ohio, where we were to play on July 24, I received a letter from him. It included a note of introduction to his girl friend. He gave me the directions to reach her house and felt that she would be interested in making my acquaintance. They were to be married in a year so I took along one of the boys and we went out and had a very nice visit. She was very interested in our experiences in Cuba. Some of our experiences through the Midwest were especially interesting. Keep in mind that the show was made up of many different people, of many nationalities. Show people are not always very careful of their actions, and although you find a lot of good people in show business, you also find some bad ones.

I remember the year we had a one-day stand in Peridishon [Prairie du Chien], Wisconsin. This was the town where they made pearl shell buttons and the streets were covered with pieces of these shells. On a sunshiny day the streets were so bright that it was hard on one's eyes, and the shells were so thick in some places that our horses kept slipping. This happened several times during our morning parade. The town was very pretty and there was hardly any dust, thanks to the shells. This was the whitest street that I have seen in any of my travels and coupled with what happened there, I remember it most vividly.

We unloaded on the west side of town and put up our tents on the east side before the morning parade at ten-thirty. I went back into town to look around and it was literally filled to the brim with people. We had an enormous crowd at the afternoon show and when it was over a bunch of us left the grounds and went to a beer garden saloon that was in the east part of town. The town had put on a lot of extra police for the day to control the crowds. One of the new deputies was a young fellow that I found out later had been working in a cigar store.

Some of the boys in the saloon were sort of cutting up and showing off a little, which created a bit of noise. The young police officer decided he would make the boys be quiet. I guess he figured he could make those boys in the saloon act like they were in church. He stepped up to the crowd of show boys, flashed his star, and told them if they didn't quiet down he would put them in the cooler. They knew they had done nothing wrong, and one of the boys in the crowd named Fred Striker, who was a bit high-tempered, got up and tried to kick the deputy out of the joint.

The deputy started backing up and then pulled out his revolver. By that time he was out on the boardwalk in front of the saloon. He kept backing down this boardwalk with Striker right after him. The show boys kept trying to get Striker to come back in, but he kept on going. The deputy fired and hit Striker in the arm, and the blood just poured out on the walk, but Striker kept after him. I was coming down the walk and heard the shot, so I stepped off it. I looked up and saw Striker bleeding badly and he hollered for me to pick up something and knock the deputy in the head. I looked around and found a rock and as I was bending over to pick it up the deputy shot again. This time it hit Striker in the shoulder, and after he shot, the deputy turned and stuck the revolver in my face and told me to drop the rock. When the shot hit Striker, it turned him around and slowed him up some but he kept coming on. By then I had dropped the rock and the deputy turned and shot Striker again. This put him down and the boys grabbed him and rushed him back to the show ground and got the doctor.

The wounds were not serious if the blood could be stopped, but it looked like Striker would bleed to death. In the excitement the deputy got away. Quite a number of the boys went back looking for him and some one told them he had gone into the corner saloon. They went to the saloon but the saloon-keeper told them he wasn't there. They ran into a bunch of police and the mayor of the town. I do not know why the other police never came up with the deputy that shot Striker. The officers told the boys that the mayor was there to talk to them about a street fight. About that time things started popping and someone hit the mayor in the face with a big belt and the buckle almost smashed his face in. All of the boys were very sorry about this but most of us never knew who did it. The mayor was a fine man and he had his daughter with him. She said a few words and was very nice about it.

When no one was arrested and the fight died down, we all went back to the show grounds. Now Buffalo Bill generally took a nap after the afternoon show, but when we got back he had already heard about Striker and the fight and I guess someone explained it to him in a way that made him mad. Buffalo Bill sent his plain-clothes men down to see what they could find out. When they returned they reported the situation was bad. It would have been all right if they had let things go after the first fight, but when the mayor got hurt everyone was very upset. We heard that the townspeople were coming down to clean up the show. Buffalo Bill was really mad when he heard this. He was the type of person you didn't make threats against. I know this to be true because at one show I remember an Englishman who started "popping off" at Buffalo Bill backstage. The next thing he knew Bill slugged him with an upper cut that knocked him to the floor. I was close and have never heard a hit that sounded as loud as that one. Bill then went into the arena to put on his act, just as calm as nothing had happened.

When Buffalo Bill heard the report that the town was going to clean him out, he told the boys there would be no night show. He also said it would take more than that little town to clean up on the show. He gave everybody orders to get their guns and those who didn't have guns to get tent pegs. He then lined up the cannons and he sent word for the people to come on out if they wanted to. We waited around and nothing happened.

After awhile, people started taking down tents and moving around real fast. We got orders to load up the buffalo and horses. I didn't know what was going on, but some of the boys remarked that we were pulling out and that Buffalo Bill was losing his nerve. We soon found out that we were leaving for Illinois and our next scheduled performance. Buffalo Bill wanted to get over the state line as soon as possible because the town had called out the state militia. We made the state line before they got there, but the boys who had taken part in the disturbance had already left the show by then. It was a good thing, too, because detectives showed up the next day and started looking for them. Striker was in the hospital and was finally released but was not prosecuted. I've thought about this incident many times during my life and considered myself lucky I didn't get mixed up any deeper in it. If I had hit that deputy and knocked him down, the boys would have tromped him to death and I would have been to blame.

When I think about the orders we got to fight the people from town, I could never see how we were going to make much of a fight at all. I guess it was mostly just a bluff since most of us only had blank shells for our guns. A few of the boys may have had live cartridges, but I can't imagine how a fight like that would have turned out.

In general, Billy's recollection of events coincides with newspaper reports. When the afternoon show ended at about 5 P.M. on August 20, 1900, the many local saloons along busy Bluff Street in Prairie du Chien offered a place where performers could relax. In one, witnesses say saloon owner Charles Staben's impatience about payment of a bar tab started a heated argument, and Staben pulled a revolver on some of the show's cowboy performers. A struggle for the weapon quickly turned into an all-out brawl, and when part-time policeman Thomas Vavra showed up, several of the "cowboy showmen" chased him into the street and began throwing rocks at him. Vavra, according to newspaper accounts, turned and fired at his pursuers. Although eyewitnesses disagree about the number of shots fired, Vavra hit at least one innocent bystander as well as a performer, apparently the man that Billy identifies as "Fred Striker."

By then, men were spilling out of every saloon on the street, some joining a throng that chased Vavra into another local watering hole. When
they couldn't find him inside, they "smashed everything they could get
their hands on." When town Marshal Charles Linder arrived on the
scene, the mob beat him, and an officer who came to his aid, to the
ground. The town mayor was not a victim of this attack as Billy had
recalled.

When the melee in Bluff Street first started, Prairie du Chien's district attorney wired Wisconsin governor Edward Scofield for troops to
quell the riot. Within five minutes, Governor Scofield responded that
he would send them, and in a second telegram he asked for help from
Buffalo Bill Cody. That message was delivered to Cody at the show-
grounds where he was taking a nap, unaware of the happenings downtown. Cody immediately called for his horse, "strapped on his belt with
two pistols at his side, and rode down Bluff Street, shouting and using
a whistle to attract his men."

Cody's startling appearance caused the crowd to disperse, and the
showmen returned to their grounds to prepare for the evening performance.
This prompted town officials to send another telegram canceling the
request for troops. By then, reported the newspaper, "the saloons closed
their doors, evidently satisfied that they exhausted the possibility for pleasure and profit incident to an occasion to which they had been liberal con-
tributors."

Although Buffalo Bill may have considered canceling the evening performance because of the street brawl, perhaps even giving orders to strike
the tents, the 7 P.M. show did go on. And, contrary to Billy's memory, performances were given in three other Wisconsin towns on subsequent days,
before the troupe left the state.

In the 1900 Route Book for Buffalo Bill's Wild West Show, a
brief journal entry minimizes the incident, places blame on a local law
officer, and claims two showmen were shot. It states: "A drunken deputy
sheriff caused a good-sized row Monday evening, by pulling a gun on some
of the riders. All hands instantly jumped in, and in the general excitement, Chas. Triangel and Harry Cinq-Mars, both of the artillery detachment, were shot. Some badly-scared local authority telegraphed for the

militia, but the trouble quickly ended and the performance went on as usual."

While it would not be unusual for the publicity-conscious Buffalo Bill to downplay the gravity of the episode, even Prairie du Chien's newspaper equivocated in blaming Cody's cowboy performers: "It is not at all certain that all the police officers engaged in the affair were themselves perfectly sober. Aside from the effect of mixing bad blood with poor whiskey, it is unlikely that there would be any friction between the show people and their patrons."

Town marshal Linder and the officer who went to his aid later recovered from their injuries. The innocent bystander hit by Officer Vavra's stray bullet also recovered, as did the cowboy performer identified by Billy as "Fred Striker." Prairie du Chien's city council refused to pay the saloon owners' claims for property damages.[9]

Naturally, there were many unusual incidents that occurred during our long cross-country train trips and performances in both small towns and large cities. There are certain things about the excitement of show business that seems to get in your blood, and at every rodeo or circus I attend, I have the urge to get down into that sawdust show ring and live those days all over again, but even with the glamour and excitement, it's not something I'd want to do all my life.

There's another incident I'd like to relate about our show tour that happened at Saginaw, Michigan. It was a big lumber town and it was quite a sight to see the rafts of logs coming down the river to the sawmills. We held the show on the west side of town and everywhere you looked there were big piles of lumber stacked around for seasoning.

Bad luck gave us a real good whack in Saginaw because Johnny Franz, one of our cowboys, took a fall with his horse and it broke him up quite a bit. Then, when the show was about over, an entire section of seats fell, hurting several spectators. One woman got a broken neck and another suffered a broken leg. This accident cost the show plenty.

Then, that afternoon, one of the boys was in town celebrating and got into some sort of trouble. Some police officers came looking for him just as we were loading up after the night show. I knew he had not been at the performance that night, but didn't think much about it with all the other things going on. This man was an Oklahoman named Henry Meagher.

Henry Meagher, a former Rough Rider in Oklahoma's Troop D, was wounded in both shoulders in the battle of Santiago, Cuba, on July 1, 1898. He was the son of John Meagher and nephew of Mike Meagher, twin brothers who served on the Wichita police force in the early 1870s. John Meagher served as Sedgwick County, Kansas, sheriff in 1874 and '75, and later moved his family to the area of Indian Territory that later became El Reno, Oklahoma.[10]

The officers followed us down to the train to look for Meagher there. Henry didn't show up but had sent his horse down for loading with another of the cowboys. They looked all through the cars but couldn't find him and finally gave up and left. It turned out that Henry had donned war paint and had been with the Indians during their act. When they finished he went right on down to the train with them. The officers had walked within a few feet of him when they were searching but the war paint and blanket had them fooled. After the train pulled out, Henry thought the officers were still on it and we never told him any different. That kept him real scared and he had to sleep with the Indians that night.

At the end of the 1901 season, I decided to quit the Buffalo Bill show and came back to Oklahoma.

PART II

1902–1961

Authors' Note: *Billy's first-person account encompasses that part of his life from 1898, when he joined the Rough Riders, to the fall of 1901, when he left the Buffalo Bill show and returned to Oklahoma. Although he wrote brief descriptions of two unrelated personal experiences after that period, we have incorporated that information as part of our own narrative covering the remainder of his life.*

CHAPTER 7

Back Home in Oklahoma

AFTER three years of near-constant travel for a mere twenty dollars per month, the excitement of performing with the Buffalo Bill show lost its appeal for Billy, and he returned to Oklahoma. At heart, he considered himself a working cowboy, and if ever he was to make it as a rancher, thirty years of age was none too soon to start.

Although he had turned down several previous offers from Rough Rider pals to enter the cattle business, the well-to-do George Knoblauck, a fellow soldier in K Troop, who was a member of the New York Stock Exchange and a brother to Charley Knoblauck, made a proposal Billy could not refuse. Believing cattle prices were about to soar, Knoblauck wanted Billy to raise a herd for him on Oklahoma range. In early November 1901, they met in Sapulpa, Indian Territory, about forty miles east of Ingalls, signed a partnership agreement, and bought four hundred head of cattle for thirty-five dollars a head. Billy had already leased several acres of Indian land along Polecat Creek, a few miles southwest of Sapulpa, where they turned the herd loose to graze while the two of them set out to find a suitable ranch in western Oklahoma.

They traveled to Higgins in the Texas Panhandle, then southeast down the Canadian River into western Oklahoma, where they found the rolling prairie to be a stockman's paradise. There were very few settlers, plenty of water, and the undulating sea of bunch and buffalo grass stretched for miles. Billy and Knoblauck each purchased 150 acres in what was then

Day County (later Ellis County), near the mouth of Packsaddle Creek. When they returned to Sapulpa, Knoblauck put Billy in charge of their cattle and went back to New York.

Within a couple of days, Billy and some hired hands started driving the herd west toward their new ranch. During the 350-mile journey to Day County, he traded a few cows for mule colts, each time making a little money. When Knoblauck arrived at the ranch later, he never questioned Billy about his free-lance trading for the mule colts, trusting instead that it would benefit their partnership. As it turned out, the mule colt trading eventually helped cut some of their losses.

For almost a year, Billy lived in a dugout and looked after their cattle, which thrived on the rich grasslands bordering the Canadian River. Then, in the fall of 1902, he got a case of homesickness about the same time he received news that the Buffalo Bill show was scheduled to perform in Guthrie. Anxious to visit with his old friends from the show and to see his girl friend, too, he left for Guthrie in early October.

Billy had been courting Mary Emily "Mollie" Pickering of Ingalls for almost three years by then. Their courtship began when she was sixteen and he was home during the off-season of the Buffalo Bill show. From then on, they had corresponded regularly and saw each other whenever they could. Before leaving Day County, Billy sent word for Mollie to meet him in Guthrie, and on the afternoon of October 8, 1902, they took in the Wild West show's performance in the territorial capital. That evening they were married by a local justice of the peace.[1]

Mollie was the oldest daughter of Dr. Jacob Hiram Pickering, a physician in the little town of Ingalls, about ten miles east of Stillwater. Dr. Pickering, his wife Charlotte Ann, and their four children had moved to the territory from Nebraska in 1893 when Mollie was only nine years old. Ingalls, established during Oklahoma's 1889 land run, had been large enough within a year to warrant a post office. Like most Oklahoma towns, Ingalls experienced rapid growth after the land opening, and by 1893 the little community had four or five physicians,

Billy and Mollie Pickering McGinty following their marriage in 1902. Courtesy of the Oklahoma Historical Society.

along with a variety of stores, livery barns, saloons, and a couple of hotels.[2]

Dr. Pickering started keeping a diary when he arrived in Oklahoma. According to Pickering, the notorious Bill Doolin outlaw gang began hanging out in Ingalls in July 1893. Doolin, who once rode with the Dalton gang, had formed his own outlaw band after the Daltons were virtually wiped out during their October 1892 raid of Coffeyville, Kansas. "As a rule," Pickering wrote in his diary, "They were quite [*sic*] and peaceable. They all went heavily armed and constantly on their guard, generally went two together. They boarded at the O.K. Hotel, staid [*sic*] at B. Dunn's [ranch one mile southeast] when not in town."[3]

Bill Doolin, George "Bitter Creek" Newcomb, Roy "Arkansas Tom" Daugherty, Dan "Dynamite Dick" Clifton,

William "Tulsa Jack" Blake, and Bill Dalton primarily engaged in drinking and poker while in town. Even so, most people considered them "well-behaved" because they sometimes attended local dances and other town functions. As one resident commented years later, "In that day, no one took any sides, nor seldom was it asked where a man came from." So it was in Ingalls.

Billy, who had moved back to Ingalls in August 1893, had been acquainted with members of the Doolin gang for some time. In 1888, before Bill Doolin and "Bitter Creek" Newcomb turned to outlawry, Billy had worked with them at the Bar X Bar Ranch, southeast of the Pawnee Indian Reservation near the confluence of the Cimarron and Arkansas Rivers. The Bar X Bar had one of the largest pastures then under lease from the Indians. With the Cimarron as its southern boundary, it stretched for seventy-five miles along the river. Billy described Bill Doolin as a slow, gander-eyed, red-haired fellow over six feet tall, who grinned very little but turned into a regular comedian when he got started. "He had huge hands," remembered Billy. They could wrap "almost twice around the butt of a six-shooter, and he was an excellent shot."

Billy had once helped Doolin unload some steers at the Red Fork station, the end of a spur on the Frisco Railroad that ran southwest from Vinita through Tulsa and across the Arkansas River. It was there he first met another Bar X Bar cowboy named George Newcomb, who was being called "Bitter Creek" by the other hands. "He had come from a good Kansas family," remembered Billy, "but got into some kind of trouble and changed his name."[4]

A couple of years later, Billy became acquainted with a soft-spoken cowhand named Roy Daugherty. At the time, Billy was in charge of a herd that belonged to Texas cattleman T. J. McElroy, whose steers were pastured on the Box T range just east of the Texas Panhandle where Ivanhoe Creek empties into Wolf Creek (near present-day Shattuck in Woodward County). It was September 1892, and Billy and several other cowhands were holding the herd in a little canyon until McElroy returned from finding a buyer in Kansas City.

When a late summer thunderstorm rolled through one night, the frightened herd stampeded and the cowboys gave chase. Luckily, Billy was riding his best night horse, "Little Neenah," who took the storm like a veteran. As lightning flashed and thunder rolled across the prairie, Billy and Little Neenah finally caught up with the leaders after a long run, but in the attempt to turn them, Little Neenah's hoofs struck the edge of an embankment and both Billy and his horse tumbled to the bottom of a shallow ravine.

Billy said he was in a real "fix" because his slicker got tangled up in the saddle horn and he had one leg pinned beneath the horse. He struggled for several minutes to get loose, and finally they both got up, wet and muddy but none the worse for wear. About then, the storm passed on and the cattle could be heard bawling all across the distant hills, too badly scattered to be rounded up that night.

The next morning there were several cattle outfits out combing the prairie for stampeded cows. While Billy and his hands searched for their TJM stock, they ran into another trail crew looking for strays wearing the Long H brand. This crew had been holding nearly three thousand longhorns about ten miles south of the Box T range when the storm hit.

With them was a young cowboy named Roy Daugherty. Slender, dark eyed, and mustached, Roy wore the best boots, Stetson, and chaps money could buy, according to Billy. The TJM and Long H crews camped together over the next few days, and Billy came to know Roy as a hard worker, but a fellow "full of devilment." Billy recalled that Roy came from an Arkansas family of preachers and had run away from home at age fourteen to become a cowboy.[5]

A few months later, when Billy returned to live in Ingalls during the summer of 1893, he again ran into Roy Daugherty, as well as Bill Doolin and "Bitter Creek" Newcomb. By then, Daugherty was being called "Arkansas Tom" and was riding

Roy "Arkansas Tom" Daugherty, former cowboy turned outlaw. CSCPA Collection.

with Doolin's outlaw gang. Earlier that same summer, the Doolin bunch had robbed a Santa Fe train near Cimarron, Kansas. The outlaws split up and Bill Doolin made his way into Ingalls and took refuge at Mary Pierce's O.K. Hotel. There, Billy and Mrs. Pierce tended to a nasty foot wound that Doolin suffered in the robbery, although at the time they didn't know how the injury was inflicted. Although Billy remained on friendly terms with members of the "Wild Bunch," as newspapers sometimes called the gang, he refused several bids to join up with them. In fact, he tried to persuade "Arkansas Tom" to leave the gang, and on one occasion had called Tom out of a drinking and poker-playing spree in an Ingalls saloon to warn him he was "in bad company."[6]

Billy was out of town taking care of some horses on September 1, 1893, a day that would be remembered for one of the Old West's deadliest gunfights between outlaws and lawmen. In his diary, Dr. Pickering described the "Battle of Ingalls," which left nearly twice as many men dead as did the much heralded fight at Tombstone's OK Corral.

The entire Doolin gang was in town that late summer day. "Arkansas Tom" occupied a second-story room of the O.K. Hotel, an establishment sometimes populated by wilted flowers of negotiable affection. The rest of the outlaws played cards and lounged about Ransom & Murry's Saloon. Pickering wrote: "On the morning of September first, 27 deputy marshals piloted into town in covered wagons. They caused no suspicion as there was [*sic*] hundreds of 'boomers' moving the same way."[7]

In fact, there were two covered wagons and a buggy containing handpicked lawmen from the county seat of Stillwater and the capital at Guthrie. The group included constables, sheriffs' deputies, and deputy U.S. marshals. Initially, thirteen officers arrived between 10:00 and 11:00 A.M., the others coming in later. They intended to surprise and capture Doolin and his men, a plan that was anything but successful.

The fight started shortly after officers took up positions at several points around town. When "Bitter Creek" Newcomb left the saloon and mounted his horse, lawman Dick Speed stepped from the shadows of a nearby building and asked a local youngster standing on the street, "Who is that rider?" His reply was, "That's Bitter Creek." The wary Newcomb heard the question and immediately went for his gun but Speed triggered the first shot, his bullet hitting Newcomb's rifle magazine and ricocheting into his groin. The wounded outlaw spurred his horse out of town as a furious firefight erupted between officers and the rest of the outlaws barricaded in the saloon.

Outnumbered and knowing that the lawmen could eventually surround them, Doolin and his men made a daring break for freedom. They burst through the tavern's side door and dashed toward their stabled horses in a livery barn up the street as "Arkansas Tom" lay down deadly cover fire from his sniper's perch on the upper floor of the O.K. Hotel. Amid a hail of bullets, Doolin, Dalton, "Dynamite Dick," and "Tulsa Jack" managed to mount up and ride out of Ingalls.

For close to four more hours, "Arkansas Tom" exchanged random shots with the officers while Dr. Pickering and at least two other local physicians dashed about town treating the wounded, which included several innocent bystanders. The doctor recorded: "I took him [the wounded Frank Briggs] to my cave [storm shelter] and dressed his wound, then went to Walker [a wounded saloon customer] and gave him Temporary aid, from there to Murry's [saloon owner] & laid his wound open and removed the shattered bone. Some of the doctors wanted me to amputate but I fought for his arm."[8]

That afternoon during a lull in the shooting, lawmen called Dr. Pickering to the hotel to talk with "Arkansas Tom." When he learned that Tom was not wounded, Pickering started to leave, but the outlaw insisted he come upstairs. According to Pickering:

> He had his coat & vest of[f] also his boots had his Winchester in his hands & revolvers lying on the bed. I said Tom come down and Surrender he says I can't do it for I wont get justis he says where is the boys [the other outlaws] I told him they had gone. He said he did not think they would leave him it hurt him bad I never seen a man wilt so in my life.[9]

"Arkansas Tom" remained in the hotel until about 2:00 P.M., then surrendered to a local preacher and was taken into custody.

The gunfight was over, but Pickering's involvement was not. He recalled that the outlaws stayed close to town, hiding out with "Bitter Creek," who was unable to travel. Pickering said he loaned Dr. John Bland, of nearby Cushing, some instru-

A replica, built in the 1920s, of the "OK Hotel," far right, where "Arkansas Tom" made his stand, is one of the few surviving buildings in Ingalls, Oklahoma. Authors' Collection.

ments to work on the outlaw's wounds, but that he personally did not know of the gang's location.

All told, the Ingalls debacle claimed the lives of five people. Lawmen Dick Speed, Lafe Shadley, and T. J. Hueston all died from the fighting; resident Dal Simmons was mistakenly shot and killed by an outlaw; and a bar customer named Walker died within days of the fight. The many wounded included saloon owners Ransom and Murry. Stray bullets, meanwhile, felled several horses and mules and caused considerable property damage all over town.[10]

Dr. Pickering, who wrote the only eyewitness account of the gunfight, practiced medicine in Ingalls for several more years and died following a brief illness in 1911 at the age of fifty-six. Local townspeople and those from miles around attended his funeral in Stillwater on May 16. He was buried in the Ingalls community cemetery.[11]

Only two weeks after the gun battle at Ingalls, the Cherokee Outlet (sometimes called Cherokee Strip) was opened for settlement by land run.[12] The morning of September 16, 1893, dawned to clear skies and a cool, brisk north wind, a welcome relief to the stifling heat wave of previous weeks. Billy enjoyed the fresh breeze in his face as he rode to the starting line northeast of Ingalls. After trail herding and working for ranching outfits in several states and territories during the last few years, he was looking forward to finally having a place of his own. His sights were set on staking a 160-acre claim along Camp Creek, a nice little spot he knew of on the old Bar X Bar range.

When army rifles barked to signal the start of the land run at high noon, Billy spurred his cow pony northward. The place he wanted was only six miles away, and although he arrived there first, another man soon rode up and started putting down stakes on the same property. Rather than fight it out, Billy figured his best bet was to file his claim first at the Perry Land Office, but once there he faced a three-day wait in line. Bewildered by the disorder and delays over land claims, he sold his place in line for thirty-five dollars and rode to Pawnee.

There, he purchased a couple of town lots and opened up a livery stable with a man named Birch. On January 23, 1894, Billy was looking after his livery business when "Tulsa Jack" Blake and other members of the Bill Doolin outfit rode into Pawnee and relieved the Farmers' and Citizens' Bank of over two hundred dollars at gunpoint. They undoubtedly would have taken more, but their raid occurred near closing time and the bank vault's new time lock had already clicked on.

The bandits left town in a flurry of gunfire, shooting out store windows as they rode from the town square northwest toward Black Bear Creek. Billy recognized "Tulsa Jack" and a couple of others, but, of course, "Arkansas Tom" was not among them. Billy had surely been right about Tom keeping bad company. By then he was serving hard penitentiary time for the Ingalls shootout nearly five months earlier. At the time, Billy never imagined that their paths would cross again in the coming years.[13]

After their marriage at Guthrie that afternoon of October, 8, 1902, Billy and Mollie were invited to ride the Buffalo Bill show train to Oklahoma City for the next day's performance. The cast not only gave the newlyweds a noisy chivaree during the trip but tried persuading them to sign up with the show for the next season. Billy's old buddies finally talked him in to riding a bronc during the Oklahoma City performance, but as soon as the show ended, he and Mollie slipped away to be alone for a while. It was a short honeymoon, and ranch life in Day County awaited them both.

By the time they arrived on their spread in western Oklahoma, George Knoblauck had built a nice little ranch house for them. Billy and Mollie put up a sign that said, "The Crossed Sabers Ranch," a rather lofty name for their humble operation, but they had big ideas for their new start in life. Billy's first priority was more pasture, so he bought two sections of school land and fenced it off. To help pay the bills, he went back to work as a Day County deputy sheriff under James L. "Doc" Smith, a job he had started during his first year there.[14]

Working as a deputy sheriff required Billy to spend some of his time in the county seat town of Grand, about sixteen miles from his ranch. The town was located in a little grove of trees near the river, and along its main street, which barely stretched three blocks, were a couple of saloons and general stores, as well as two newspapers, a livery stable, and the two-story Grand Hotel, the most popular meeting place in town. The main water supply came from a spring on a nearby hill, prompting people to remark that Grand was the only town in Oklahoma where you climbed for water. In its heyday Grand boasted only about one hundred inhabitants, most of whom were county officials and lawyers. The legal business seemed always to prosper in territorial towns because the courts were clogged with "contests" over settler claims.[15]

Billy and Mollie both learned quite a bit about ranching during their first year together in Day County, and Billy found out some things about Mollie, too. He already knew she was a good rider, practically growing up on horseback while making the rounds through the countryside with her physician-father when she was a little girl. He was not surprised that she frequently saddled her own horse and made the long ride from their ranch to Grand, but he was unaware, until living there awhile, that she was practically fearless.

One day Billy and a fellow deputy named Billy Wicks were sent out to collect back taxes from a local rancher. The man owned over four hundred ponies, and he and Wicks had orders to round up just enough of them to cover the tax bill. Knowing that the rancher had already tried to hide most of the ponies south of the river, Billy and Wicks wanted help in finding them and Mollie was the first to volunteer. Billy wasn't too keen on the idea but since they were just looking for ponies he let her go along.

A couple of miles south of the Canadian River, they located a small bunch and Billy left Mollie there to hold them while he and Wicks rode on to look for more. That afternoon they were still searching miles away when a heavy dust and sand storm blew up. They started back in the direction of the river to find Mollie, but visibility was nil and Billy and Wicks wandered around aimlessly until after dark. Finally, the wind died down and they came across a man who pointed them in the right direction. They found Mollie and the ponies she was holding about midnight and finally headed back for their ranch against a strong north wind. Mollie told them she assumed they had just forgotten her and she had been waiting for the storm to let up before going back home on her own.

During their stay in western Oklahoma, Billy also discovered that Mollie was experienced at fighting prairie fires. He was in

Grand one day when a blaze started about thirty-five miles north of their ranch. Pushed along by a strong wind, it swept toward their place like a racehorse, the rising black cloud of smoke to the east visible for miles as he set out, as fast as he could, on the long ride to their ranch where Mollie was by herself. By the time Billy got there, the fire had already overrun their land, but Mollie was all right. She had set a backfire, saving herself, the stock, and the house. Mollie helped set a backfire once before when she was a little girl in Nebraska and a prairie fire had threatened their farm. Even then, the fire still came dangerously close but she and her family were able to save the horses and cows by bringing them up to the house and holding on to them by ropes through the windows.

Billy and Mollie's first son, Delmar, was born on August 29, 1903. In the fall of that year, just before the end of his second year in partnership with George Knoblauck, Billy shipped some of their cattle to market. He was not surprised that they sold for only thirteen dollars a head, a considerable loss from the thirty-five dollars a head they paid for them. The only consolation was that he had warned Knoblauck about the cattle market when they started, and the New Yorker seemed to take the loss in stride. Meanwhile, they had made a little money on the mule colts he traded for, so they decided to extend their agreement another year in hopes of better times.

By late 1904, however, rangeland became even scarcer in Day County. Cattle began drifting across the river, crowding their range, and a big herd was put in just north of their ranch. At the same time, "nesters," as Billy called them, got "as thick as blackbirds." They plowed the ground, fenced the fields, and built houses everywhere. He now considered the country unfit for cowmen, and when the year was up, he and Knoblauck dissolved their partnership. Knoblauck traded the ranch house and cattle for some lots in Guthrie, and Billy took his share in horses. A few months later, he and Mollie rode back toward Payne County, and what horses they didn't trade off along the way, they traded in Ingalls.[16]

The couple eventually settled near Ripley, a few miles south of Ingalls. Their second son, Otto Wayne ("Jack"), was born on August 6, 1906, followed by Clarence Lee ("Mac") on December 29, 1907.[17]

In 1906, Billy started work as a school land appraiser for Oklahoma government, his appointment made by Territorial Governor Frank Frantz, formerly a captain of Rough Rider Troop A. To avoid conflicts of interest, the land commission prohibited appraisers from evaluating property in their home counties, so the job required Billy to travel. Most of the time he covered counties in western Oklahoma, but he was home on weekends. He held the position for only about a year when, in the spring of 1907, he received an offer to return to show business.

A Montana bronc rider named "Kid" Gabriel was putting together a stage show as part of a traveling exhibition of paintings by western artist Frederic Remington, and Billy eagerly accepted Gabriel's offer for more money than the land-appraising job paid. The two met in Columbus, Missouri, where they had a portable rope corral made for the show. They then went to New Jersey, erected the corral on some property Gabriel had obtained, and began training their horses in it. Each day they reduced the size of the corral a little until it was only about forty by sixty-feet, the approximate size of the stage they would use.

Another act for the show involved a specially-made mechanical horse. The device appeared authentic right down to the hide and hair, and by operating some hidden levers, the "horse" could be placed in eleven different lifelike poses. The horse was snow-white and stood on a black pedestal that was surrounded by black velvet curtains. From the audience it looked like the real thing, and each time the curtain raised, Billy and Gabriel took turns on stage with the horse, striking different poses.

In the first scene, Billy sat on the ground in front of the horse, reading a letter from a nearby mailbox. The horse stood with its head down as if grazing, the rein hanging to the ground. After a few seconds, the curtain closed and then opened again, this time with "Kid" Gabriel mounted, a rope in hand ready to throw a loop. This continued for eleven different poses portraying still-life scenes of the West.

The rope corral came into play when Billy and "Kid" Gabriel rode real horses on stage, including bucking broncs. The animals were shod with rubber shoes, and a heavy, three-inch matting covered the stage floor. This unique performance opened at New York City's Vanderbilt Theatre in the spring of 1907 and marked the first time real bucking horses were ridden on stage in New York or anywhere else.[18]

Although initially successful, the show closed after only a few months. Two stock market crashes that year created the so-called panic of 1907. Money was tight and the economy took a severe downturn. When Billy returned home that winter, all the local banks had closed, but he had drawn his pay in cash before leaving New York, so the financial crisis had little effect on him. For the next two years, he stayed on his farm between Ripley and Ingalls, raising some livestock and training horses.[19]

In June of 1910, Billy was back in New York, where scores of Rough Riders from around the country gathered for a combination reunion and welcome home party for Teddy Roosevelt on his return from an extended trip overseas. While there, Billy and a few others received a special invitation to visit their former colonel's Sagamore Hill home on Long Island.

A *New York Times* story reported:

> The Rough Riders went to Sagamore Hill on an earnest mission. [Edward] Borein, McGinty and [Edwin] Emerson [A Rough Rider and war correspondent] donned their uniforms in New York at sunrise, ferried across the East River, then rode all the way to Oyster Bay on cow ponies. They bore the Rough Riders' dearest possessions, the two regimental flags which they carried in their charge up San Juan Hill.[20]

Edward Borein was a former cowboy turned artist.[21] Along with Billy and Emerson, the group included Madill McCormick of the *Chicago Tribune*; Jack Greenway of Arizona; James R. Garfield, secretary of the interior; and Gifford Pinchot, chief forester for the United States and later governor of Pennsylvania. After the presentation ceremony and dinner, Roosevelt gave the men a tour of his home. Billy took special interest in the study, estimating the room to be "about forty-foot long" with mahogany walls almost completely covered with "deer, moose, and elk horns." At one point, they went into the library where Roosevelt showed them a stack of letters about three feet high. Most had arrived during his recent trip aboard, and Roosevelt said it was his practice to answer each of them. Billy remembered one from a New York City woman who wanted to sue Roosevelt because his welcome home parade through Manhattan had created a two-hour traffic jam that delayed her for an appointment.

A few days after returning to the city, where he and other Rough Riders were staying, Billy learned there was to be a riding contest at Southampton, beginning July second. On June 30, he ferried across the East River and rode toward the ritzy Long Island tourist town to enter the event that was being billed as a "Military Circus and Wild West Show." Judges for the contest included several well-known westerners, among them Charles J. "Buffalo" Jones, whom Billy had known during his cowboy days near the Texas Panhandle's Palo Duro Canyon.

"Buffalo" Jones, of Garden City, Kansas, was a close friend of "Buffalo" Bill Cody and Gordon "Pawnee Bill" Lillie. Cody and Lillie had once been rivals, but became partners in the production of Wild West shows, and both Lillie and Jones had been instrumental in the preservation of the buffalo. Jones, an adventurer and world traveler, often journeyed overseas to capture wild animals for North American zoos. During a recent trip to Africa, he had filmed a group of cowboys as they roped wild game.[22]

The Southampton riding contest had been organized as fund raiser for a local hospital, and the *New York Times*

Billy and cowboy-turned-artist Ed Borein at the 1910 Military Circus and Bronc Riding Championship in Southampton, Long Island. Glenn D. Shirley Western Americana Collection, National Cowboy & Western Heritage Museum.

reported that "several of Colonel Roosevelt's Rough Riders" participated during the three-day affair. The bronc riding event, a fairly unique feature for easterners, was held as the grand finale each day.[23] As top prize, New York's Tiffany Jewelers donated a specially inscribed silver cup in honor of late Rough Rider William Tiffany, recognizing the winner as "World Bronc Riding Champion."

Billy was thirty-nine-years-old at the time but still extremely fit as a rider, and if nothing else, experience was on his side. He had first straddled bucking horses for a living at age fourteen. That was in 1885, southeast of Dodge City, when he worked for the Mack Mann Ranch on the old Mobeetie Stage and Freight Trail from Dodge into the Texas Panhandle.

Undoubtedly, his most memorable bronc-riding experience had been in 1900 during a Buffalo Bill show performance at

Madison Square Garden. In front of a wildly applauding, standing-room-only crowd, his horse had jumped into the front-row seats, breaking Billy's leg on a banister. After the performance, he told a newspaper reporter that men who ride broncs for a living, whether in a show or as a horse-breaker, rarely lasted more than a dozen years. By then, he had been at it for fifteen years.

If, during the Southampton contest, Billy thought back to that bone-breaking ride, it apparently held no fear for him. More than likely, he just remembered the time he worked for the Star Ranch in south Texas, where one winter he broke 413 horses by himself. In fact, never had he been thrown by a bronc before or since.[24]

After three grueling days of riding several bucking horses each afternoon, Billy ended up with top honors on July 4, winning the "ride-off," by what he called a "scratch," over Arizona cowboy Bert Bryan. The Tiffany cup won that day is still a prized possession of the McGinty family.[25]

Later that same year, Roy "Arkansas Tom" Daugherty paid a visit to the McGinty home. Tom had served fourteen years of a fifty-year sentence under federal lockup at Lansing, Kansas, and McAlester, Oklahoma, for his part in the Ingalls shootout. One of his brothers, a minister, had arranged a pardon, and after Tom reported to U.S. Deputy Marshal Bill Tilghman in Oklahoma City, he went to see Billy in Ripley. At the time, Mollie was hospitalized with a fever, and for several weeks the likable Tom did the washing and cooking for Billy and his three young sons.[26]

Tom later played himself in the 1915 silent film *The Passing of the Oklahoma Outlaws*. The movie, directed by Bill Tilghman, was billed as an accurate portrayal of outlaws and lawmen and included a scene that reenacted the Ingalls gunfight. In keeping with the tradition of the time, Tilghman went on the road with the movie, lecturing his audience from the stage and introducing Tom as the last member of the infamous Doolin gang. Tom continued to give up real-life ban-

One of Billy's several rides during the July 1910 Bronc Riding Championship at Southampton, Long Island. CSCPA Collection.

ditry for several more years but later fell in with a tough crowd. In 1916 he was involved in a bank burglary in Neosho, Missouri. He served penitentiary time in Jefferson City, was released in 1921, but teamed with three other men to rob a bank in the farming community of Asbury, Missouri, in 1923. The following summer, Joplin police detectives located Tom in the home of a friend and, rather than submit to arrest, the last of the old time Oklahoma outlaws died in a gunfight with lawmen.[27]

In 1912, Billy took on a new venture when the discovery of an oil field in Creek County east of Ripley lured people, money, and new businesses to the area. There, a little village known as Fulkerson quickly blossomed into a frenzied, rip-roaring town called Drumright, a collection of tents and ramshackle buildings set amid over three hundred oil derricks. Oklahoma's oil boom era had begun in 1901 when the first commercially successful well was drilled near Red Fork, southwest of Tulsa. For the next thirty years, oil discoveries gave rise to dozens of new towns, from Cromwell in Seminole country to Whizbang in the Osage.[28]

The drillers, rig builders, pipe layers, and lease hounds who flooded into Drumright and nearby Cushing all needed transportation, and there was good money in hauling them around. Billy heard that one man was taking in twenty-five dollars a day carrying oil field men and sightseers, so he bought a used Regal motor car and went into business as the "William M. McGinty Livery Service."

Billy soon found the Regal was not up to the task. When it rained, Drumright, built on the side of a hill, became its own teeming mudslide where nothing moved unless pulled by a mule. Even out in the flat country, the mud was so deep and the rutted roads had such high centers that nearly every car except the Model T Ford bogged down. Billy replaced the Regal with a Model T touring car. It still required a lot of upkeep for tires and wheels, but some days he cleared as much as thirty-five dollars. He worked nights, too, under a contract to meet the 2:00 A.M. train at the Cushing depot and carry legal papers, and sometimes people, to Drumright.

He operated his livery business for three years, and then, about 1916, formed a partnership with Bert Bevins, opening a subagency car dealership selling Fords in Ripley. The highly popular Model T, the first affordable car for the masses, underwent little in the way of design change through 1927. Billy and Bevins sold quite a few cars at first, but when Ford made it a requirement for subagencies to have a garage in connection with their operation, they switched to selling Dodges for a dealer out of Pawnee. Billy also dabbled in Overland model cars and had a Chevrolet dealership for a short time.[29]

During his years in the livery and automobile sales business, Billy found a very practical use for the silver Tiffany trophy cup he had won at the 1910 bronc riding championship. Billy Jay McGinty of Glencoe, Oklahoma, a grandson, recalls his grandmother telling him that Billy always carried the cup in his car, using it to fill the Model T's radiator with water from nearby creeks.[30]

With their father in the car business, Billy's three boys took up driving when they were barely old enough to reach the pedals. With his encouragement, they practiced their skills on an old wagon road through an isolated area north of the Cimarron called Ghost Hollow, a legendary spot for hanging outlaws in earlier times. Billy's son, Otto Wayne, known as Jack, was so adept at driving that in 1917, the year he turned eleven, he chauffeured a Ripley couple on their "second" honeymoon.

Sixty-five-year-old local farmer W. R. Birdwell had bought a new Model T from Billy, but didn't know how to drive it, so he asked him to let Jack drive it for him. With Billy and Mollie's consent, young Jack drove the Birdwells to Kansas for a two-week trip. When they returned, the couple was convinced of the car's reliability and hooked on the delights of touring the country, so with Jack as their trusty driver, they set out on a three-month excursion through Nebraska, Wyoming, Colorado, New Mexico, and Texas. Along their route, the Birdwells sent postcards to Jack's parents assuring them that all was well. Since there were no laws governing a driver's age or experience at the time, little thought was given to a young boy behind the wheel of a car as long as he seemed to know what he was doing. Only once did Jack get a second look when a policeman stopped the car in Denver. The officer told the Birdwells it was "OK" for young Jack to drive as long as he could "drive right."[31]

Billy left the automobile business in 1924 when Ford started dominating the market by financing their cars on a "time" plan. "Anyone could buy a Ford," said Billy, but most competitive dealers, and he was one of them at the time, were unable to sell on "time" because they "could not handle the paper." Fortunately, the same year Billy quit the automobile business, Ripley's postal service was expanded to meet the area's increasing population, and when Mollie was appointed postmistress, Billy signed on to work as her assistant.[32]

During the early 1920s, Billy also started driving a school bus for the Ripley consolidated schools; a job he held for

Billy and some of his Ripley school passengers in 1929. CSCPA Collection.

nineteen years. He carried kids of all ages, from first-graders to high schoolers, on a route that went through town and into the nearby countryside. One of the first buses he drove was considerably underpowered, and depending on the load, climbing the hill on the north side of the Cimarron River could be a challenge. Occasionally, the bus made it only about halfway up the incline, so Billy would ask the kids to get out and help push to the top. When they climbed back on, he'd let them dig into a bag of candy or peanuts he kept as a treat just for such occasions.[33]

One brisk January afternoon in 1923, Billy was taking the kids home, and while driving along Ripley's Main Street, he noticed a black sedan speeding away from the Farmers State Bank. Only moments before, the car's occupants had entered the sturdy stone building with drawn pistols, emptied the tellers' cash drawers and ordered assistant cashier Harold Straughn to open the vault. Straughn tried to bluff the bandits, telling them the safe was "on a time lock" and could not be opened.

"If you don't open it," said one of the gun-wielding robbers, "I'll blow your head off. As a matter of fact, I might do that anyway."

It did not take long for Straughn to open the vault and after they looted it of nearly $3,500, the bandits locked Straughn and a customer inside it, ran from the bank and jumped in their getaway car.

Billy drove by just in time to see the car speed off as several employees and customers ran out yelling they had been heldup. One was a man Billy knew and he told him to take over driving the school bus. Billy then retrieved a shotgun from inside the bank and when he got back outside he ran into two of his friends, U. E. Moore and C. D. Mooney. The three of them piled into a nearby car and started in pursuit of the holdup men. The chase took them north across the river and through the town of Ingalls, but Billy and his makeshift posse lost the bandits a few miles northwest of Yale when they could not get their car across a flooded country road.[34]

Robbers hit the same Ripley bank several times over the years. During an attempt in 1931, one of Billy's sons mounted a spirited defense that prevented a holdup. Twenty-four-year-old Clarence McGinty, Billy and Mollie's youngest, had been working as a cashier for a couple of years when two men wearing overalls walked in one September afternoon. Clarence remembered that the robbers had worn overalls when the bank was looted barely twelve months earlier, so when he spotted a third man outside in a car with its engine running, he knew what would happen next.

Clarence slipped into the vault, picked up a shotgun that was always stored there and listened in on the conversation at the counter only a few feet away. As expected, he heard one of the men telling the employees to throw up their hands. At that command, Clarence stepped into view, raised the shotgun and fired over the top of the tellers' cage. The shot went high but the deafening report sent everyone in the bank to the floor. The two bandits fired back toward the vault from the prone position, but Clarence had already ducked back inside. At that point the bandits jumped up and ran out the door toward the waiting getaway car, but one of them was so shaken by the shotgun-wielding bank employee that he ran past the car and down Main Street where some irate citizens disarmed him. As the other bandit reached the car and closed the door, Clarence ran to the front window and let loose with the second blast from his double-barreled shotgun, taking out the glass and peppering the getaway car with lead. The two would-be robbers left Ripley, headed south but without any money. The manhunt lasted only a few days. The following week, brothers Buell and Wayne Webb were arrested near Sapulpa, both suffering from buckshot wounds.[35]

Billy's widely varied work career over the years was driven more by opportunity than aimless drifting. He was never afraid to take a chance on something new, whether automobiles or another medium of performing. In 1925 show business beckoned him again by way of a modern contraption called radio.

It all started with some local musicians who had formed a little cowboy band in 1921. Mostly, they performed in Ripley and a few other small Oklahoma towns, playing western tunes at town dances. The band was first called "The Old Time Fiddlers," and later, "The Ripley Cowboy Band" since all the musicians came from Ripley.[36] When not giving a performance someplace, they played for their own pleasure in Ripley's barbershop. Ulys Moore, the local barber and the same man who helped Billy chase the bank robbers in 1923, and Frank Sherrill, a fiddle player who worked for the Mulberry Oil Company, were the band's founding members.

One day in early 1925, the group was practicing in a local garage where Frank Sherrill was trying to teach Billy's son Jack to harmonize with a musical instrument. When George Youngblood, the owner of Ripley's telephone exchange, came by to get Jack for a trip to nearby Bristow where they were to pick up some new radios to sell, he paused to listen for awhile. Later, as they drove toward Bristow, Youngblood casually mentioned to Jack that the band might sound good on that town's new radio station, which had gone on the air only a few weeks earlier.[37]

The rage over radio was at its peak in the mid-1920s, helping to give the decade some of its well-known "roar." The broadcasting era began in 1920 when station KDKA in Pittsburgh, Pennsylvania, received the first commercial radio station license in the United States. Commercial stations were soon cropping up everywhere, and by mid-1921, Oklahoma was on its way to becoming a leader in radio development among western states.

Transmitting from a garage in Oklahoma City, E. C. Hull and H. S. Richards, electricians turned radio enthusiasts, formed a partnership in the spring of 1921 and went on the air as amateur radio station 5XT. Initially, broadcasting was just a hobby to them, their real goal being to manufacture and sell radio receivers. In the meantime, they began a series of "wireless concerts" that consisted of playing phonograph records over 5XT each night, and when the mail began pouring in from listeners over nine hundred miles away, they knew they were on to something. In the early part of 1922, Hull and Richards applied for a commercial license and 5XT was designated WKY, becoming the twenty-eighth commercially licensed station in the United States. By the end of that year, twelve commercial radio stations were on the air in Oklahoma and four more were added in 1923. Radio fever had a firm grip on Oklahoma as well as the nation.

From crop and weather reports and baseball scores, early broadcasters soon turned to musical entertainment in the form of church choirs, local orchestras, and the latest dance tunes played from the "Victor talking machines." Once the programs gained a following, businesses could not resist buying time, and the future of commercial radio seemed limitless.

In 1925, just a few miles from Ripley, E. H. Rollestone, a young oil millionaire, investor, and civic leader with a little P. T. Barnum in his blood, began a venture to put his town of

Bristow on the broadcast map. On January 12, radio station KFRU, which, according to the station manager, stood for "Kind Friends Remember Us," fired up its 500-watt transmitter and started broadcasting from a glass-walled studio on the mezzanine of the Roland Hotel in downtown Bristow.[38]

It was on KFRU that Ripley businessman George Youngblood, an astute promoter, envisioned a performance by the Ripley Cowboy Band. Youngblood believed the band had great potential but needed an authentic cowboy to be part of it, and he figured Billy McGinty, once a real working cowboy and former Rough Rider, who was already widely known in much of the West, was just the right man. At first, Billy resisted Youngblood's pitch, but when band members, all friends of his, agreed that it would be a good thing for the town, he said "yes," lending his name to the "Billy McGinty Cowboy Band."

On March 19, 1925, Youngblood and Frank Sherrill motored over to Bristow and arranged for a forthcoming radio performance. This occurred just a few days after KFRU broadcast a musical program by some Ripley High School students. That event had prompted Ripley's local newspaper to report proudly, "There are at least twenty-five or thirty radios in Ripley homes."[39]

Billy's cowboy band made its radio debut on KFRU in early May. Youngblood, acting as promoter and announcer, introduced the members as: Frank Sherrill, first fiddler; U. E. Moore, bass player; Paul Harrison, guitar; Guy Messecar, mandolin; H. C. Hackney, banjo; Mrs. Marie Mitchell, pianist; and Ernest Bevins, harmonica. Bristow's newspaper, prone to detailed write-ups of the station's programming, reported that Bevins, only thirteen years old, played several solo selections, including "*Irish Washerwoman*, *Red Wing*, and *Casey Jones*, each being dedicated to some of his friends in regular radio procedure."

During the broadcast, Youngblood gave a little spiel about the band, but was almost overcome by "mike fright." Billy said Youngblood opened his mouth a few times and nothing came

Billy McGinty's Cowboy Band ca. 1925. Mollie is seated to Billy's right.
CSCPA Collection.

out, and then "his face turned white." Youngblood eventually
made it through his written speech, talking about each band
member and pointing out that Billy was a "real cowboy" and a
war hero to boot.

Next, it was Billy's turn to say a few words—as far as he was
concerned, the fewer the better. "I was sure scared and that
mike made me shake some," said Billy. "A kind of lump came
up in my throat and I couldn't even squawk."

When he finally did get some words out, he had no idea if
they made any sense. The band's namesake then turned from

the microphone and walked out of the studio so fast, Young-blood was left to fill "dead air," which he tried to do by calling for a quick tune from the band. Billy said it was the last time they called on him to do any talking. He had lent his name and reputation to the band, and even helped manage it, but had no intention of making speeches, and that included talks on the radio.[40]

Along with their regular broadcasts over the Bristow station, the band played other parts of Oklahoma during the summer of 1925. Mollie McGinty, who sometimes traveled with them, was one of the band's earliest vocal performers, but her singing career was confined mostly to local appearances. Usually, when the band performed outside of Ripley, substitutes were picked up to replace the original musicians, who all had regular "day" jobs and could seldom travel.

In Oklahoma City, McGinty's Cowboy Band worked from the studios of KFJF by day while appearing nightly at the Liberty Theatre. Their next stop was Tulsa, where they performed at the Mayo Hotel as part of Pawnee Bill's Indian Show. There, a local radio station manager gave the group high marks as being "the smoothest string band he had ever heard."

At one appearance, a Chicago promoter approached Billy to offer his services in helping arrange an extensive tour of Midwest states. It was evidence that the band's fame extended well outside Oklahoma, but Billy declined, explaining his group was made up of hometown boys with local obligations.[41]

In the fall of 1925, E. H. Rollestone abruptly sold KFRU's station call sign and equipment to a college in Columbia, Missouri, and began working toward creating a "super power broadcasting station." It went on the air the following year as radio station KVOO, the "Voice of Oklahoma," with studios in Tulsa and Bristow.[42] The changes made by Rollestone eventually served to enhance the band's growing popularity, increasing its audience throughout Oklahoma, and bringing more offers from eager promoters who wanted them to perform in other states.

The issue of the band touring outside of Oklahoma took care of itself late in 1925 when Stillwater's Otto Gray and his wife entered the picture to, as the *Stillwater Gazette* reported, "extend its field of action in January 1926." The creative and promotional-minded Gray brought a new dimension to the band's smooth string sound, adding vocal arrangements featuring his wife, Florence, and their son, Owen. Otto Gray and his family integrated the music and imagery of the West for the first time, pioneering a popular and enduring style. Like Billy, Gray was a former range rider and not a musician, but he had a knack for knowing what audiences wanted to hear. At first, he did the musical arranging and performed rope tricks on stage, but in time, he took over as the band's manager and announcer.

Soon after Gray had joined the group, they played a late night performance in Okmulgee, Oklahoma. Unaware of a local ordinance against it, one of the band members left his car on the street overnight and the police towed it. Thinking it had been stolen, McGinty and Gray went to the police station the next morning and were informed that the car had been impounded because of the no parking law.

The police sergeant gave them a difficult time until he learned who they were; then the three of them decided to pull a practical joke. The other band members, who were staying at a local motel, were ordered to report to the station where the police judge acted highly indignant about the parking violation. He fined them each five dollars for "disturbing the peace" during the previous night's performance, then locked them in cells. Only Billy and Gray were spared jail, supposedly so they could plead their case to the judge.

The two then retrieved the band instruments from the motel and returned to the station. When the judge called the "prisoners" back into court, he told them they could "play their way out of jail." Billy said it "took a couple of minutes for the boys to realize it was a joke," but after everyone had a good laugh they tuned up their instruments and gave a little performance right there in the Okmulgee police station.[43]

By the turn of 1926, Gray had booked the band for a two-week stand at the Orpheum Theatre in Kansas City, starting in late January. At the time they were still performing at a little theatre in Hominy, Oklahoma, only a few miles from Ripley, and when that engagement ended, no one was very surprised that the musicians all resigned because of responsibilities that prevented extensive travel on a regular basis.

For a time, Billy remained associated with Otto Gray and the new musicians. Although Gray took over as the band's manager, Billy continued to lend his name as before. He enjoyed traveling, meeting people, and talking about old times. In so doing, he was a good promoter for the group, but he drew the line at formal speechmaking. Mollie also went on the road, occasionally appearing on stage to sing a ballad or two. Having played the piano since she was a little girl, she knew music and had developed into a capable vocalist. Her family recalls Mollie's love for singing everything from church hymns to popular tunes.

By the spring of 1926, notices and news stories about the group listed Otto Gray as official manager and announcer for "McGinty's Cowboy Band," which, by then, had been slightly downsized to include only one violin, a mandolin, guitar, piano, and a bass cello.[44]

Under Gray's guidance, the group swiftly gained fame as the country's first nationally recognized cowboy band. During a tour of the Midwest in April, they received rave reviews for a performance on broadcast powerhouse WLW in Cincinnati, Ohio,[45] and in Springfield, Illinois, carmaker Henry Ford saw them play and made national headlines when he gave his "stamp of approval to Oklahoma cowboy music." His comments were carried in a wire service story that was passed along from Tulsa's KVOO, the band's "flagship" station.[46]

On one road trip, Gray reported to the *Stillwater Gazette* that they had traveled two thousand miles since leaving Oklahoma, and only "forty-nine miles of the trip had been on dirt roads." By the fall of 1926, their popularity had grown, gener-

Billy (holding a rope at left) and his cowboy band on tour with their travel bus ca. 1926. Glenn D. Shirley Western Americana Collection, National Cowboy & Western Heritage Museum.

ating thousands of letters and cards of appreciation mailed to Gray's Stillwater home.[47] The requests for recording sessions, theatre appearances, and radio performances made for an increasingly demanding schedule, but the money rolled in, too. Billy and the group traveled in a caravan of fancy, custom-built automobiles, including a three-ton sedan that looked like a railroad observation car. Beyond their glitzy cars and flashy cowboy outfits, however, what set them apart was their wide repertory of western, country, and sentimental parlor songs, performed and promoted in a fashion that placed them among the originators of today's country-and-western music style.[48]

By the late 1920s, the little band from Payne County had become so popular that it was heard on 130 radio stations across the country, including regular appearances on NBC's "Red" and "Blue" networks. The near-constant traveling was too much for Billy, however, and by 1928 he decided it was high time to stay home and take up activities more suitable to his nearly sixty years of age. The band he had helped start toward national fame, meanwhile, continued to hold the public spotlight through the mid-1930s under the new name "Otto Gray and His Oklahoma Cowboys."[49]

CHAPTER 8

To the Last Man

ONCE he stopped traveling with the band, Billy was able to spend even more time on his little farm in Ripley, where one bright spring day in May 1932 his reputation as a trainer and bronc rider got tarnished a bit. He had saddled a horse in his backyard and just mounted up when it suddenly reared, then sidestepped, slamming him against a cement pillar. Still robust and resilient, even at age sixty-one, Billy managed to stay aboard the bucking horse until it suddenly made a mad dash under a clothesline and raked him off its back. The mishap temporarily put him out of action with three broken ribs and numerous bruises.[1]

By September he had mended well enough to direct the Old Settlers' Reunion, a late-summer celebration held annually near Perkins, beginning in 1922. The Old Settlers consisted of men and women who had participated in any of Oklahoma's several land openings, but in the region of the state where Billy lived, the reunion primarily involved the early pioneers from Payne and surrounding counties. In addition to Billy, other key members of this group included former cowboy Bert Frame, on whose ranch the event was held; early-day army scout and range rider Frank Orner, who homesteaded near Perkins in 1889 and later served in the state legislature; and the irrepressible Frank "Pistol Pete" Eaton, whose caricatured image later served as the official mascot for Oklahoma State University. Billy ran the reunion entertainment program like a typical performance of Buffalo Bill's Wild West show. Following an opening parade, he

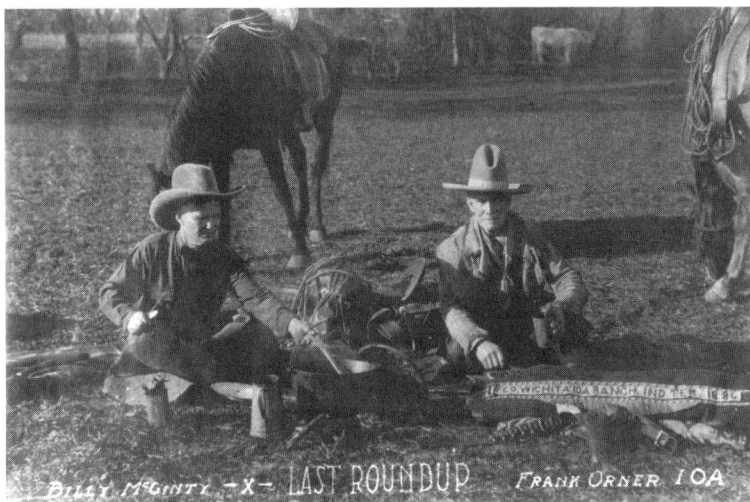

Billy McGinty and Frank C. Orner re-create a roundup scene at the 1932 Old Settlers' Reunion near Perkins, Oklahoma. McGinty represented the Bar X Bar and Orner the IOA, ranches where both men once worked prior to opening the territory to settlers. Orner served as secretary-treasurer and historian of the Old Settlers' Association and was active in the Oklahoma Historical Society. CSCPA Collection.

staged several exciting acts, including an Indian attack on a stagecoach, the rustling and branding of cattle, and the hanging of a horse thief.[2]

A couple of years before the Old Settlers' group was established, Billy became a charter member of the Cherokee Strip Cowpunchers Association. Joe Miller, eldest of the Miller brothers, conceived the idea in 1920, sending invitations to all the old cowboys he could recall who had once worked the cattle ranges of the Cherokee Outlet prior to its opening for settlement in 1893. Miller brought them together at his 101 Ranch in Bliss (later Marland), Oklahoma. Most had not seen each other since the early cattle-drive days, and when they met on Cowboy Hill, a high bank overlooking the Salt Fork River near the 101 Ranch headquarters, they decided to make the reunions an annual affair each September. Billy helped to

Billy, decked out in gear from his range rider days, at the 1941 Old Settlers' Reunion near Perkins, Oklahoma. CSCPA Collection.

organize the group whose only bylaws wisely stated they would meet yearly without any discussion of politics or religion. The annual dues were set at one dollar. Billy remained a life-long member.

In 1930 Zack Miller, the surviving member of the Miller brother trio, donated the parcel of land on Cowboy Hill for the group's permanent meeting place and the men constructed a building and campsite facilities there. In the years that followed, the aging cowboys, the last of a dying breed, met to reminisce with old friends and enjoy the dances, picnics, and rodeo that highlighted the annual three-day celebration. Billy and his family attended almost every year, and beginning in the late 1940s, Mollie took over the secretary's position for the CSCPA auxiliary, made up of the men's wives. She kept the group's records for several years before Bessie McGinty, one of Billy's daughters-in-law, assumed the role.

Among the elite members of the CSCPA were several well-known men from Oklahoma and the West, including early-day deputy U.S. marshal and prominent Oklahoma City business-man Charles Colcord; outlaw hunter and former U.S. marshal of Oklahoma Territory William D. Fossett; former Pinkerton detective Charley Siringo; Wild West showman and rancher Gordon "Pawnee Bill" Lillie; Bill Pickett, rodeo champion and inventor of the bull-dogging event; and range rider Rolla Goodnight, the nephew of Charles Goodnight, noted ranch-man of Palo Duro Canyon, Texas.

In addition to their own reunions, the old cowboys were honored at Enid and other towns during yearly events cele-brating the opening of the Cherokee Outlet. Billy and his fel-low old-timers always rode at the head of the parade, side by side, just as they had done in the days of cattle trailing. With the help of CSCPA members, the state of Oklahoma established the exact location of the old Chisholm Cattle Trail in the late 1930s, making it possible to mark the famed route from the Red River to Caldwell, Kansas.

In 1937, Billy put some of his life experiences in print by publishing a short volume entitled *The Old West*. Only 1,000 copies of the 108-page booklet were printed, most of which he gave to his friends and admirers, but the stories were so popu-lar that the *Ripley Review* ran them as a newspaper series in 1937 and 1938. By then, he had started working on a book manuscript titled "Adventure Trail." With the help of *Review* editor Glenn L. Eyler, it too, was published as a local newspa-per series of the same name. Billy wrote not only about his days as a Rough Rider and Wild West show performer but also about his 1938 vacation through parts of Old Mexico, colorfully describing everything from the country's historical sights and political climate to bull fighting.[3]

Even as he got along in years, Billy was the exception to those unyielding old-timers who declared they had seen many changes in their lifetime and had been against every one of them. Instead, he embraced technological progress while hold-

ing fast to the history and values of his cowboy heritage.
Although the Old West had long since disappeared, Billy kept
his memories of those days alive through his newspaper writing
and his involvement with the Cherokee Strip Cowpunchers
Association and the Old Settlers. He also collected hundreds of
mementos from his years as a cowhand, Rough Rider, and Buffalo Bill show performer, displaying them in an old building
behind his Ripley home that served as sort of a makeshift
museum.[4]

Of all his experiences, however, serving as a Rough Rider was
his greatest source of pride, probably because so few could
make that claim. Likewise, visiting with the "Boys of '98," his
comrades in arms, who regularly gathered at reunions until all
of them were gone, became his greatest enjoyment.

Although not considered a crucial conflict, the Spanish-
American War was a major turning point for America. By 1898,
Cuba had been struggling for independence from Spain for several decades, and U.S. political leaders began viewing the island
as an opportunity for economic exploitation, a country need-
ing American control. At the same time, rival New York newspapers served up sensationalized accounts of Spanish atrocities
against Cubans that included starvation and torture. This "yellow journalism," reflected in newspapers nationwide, had an
incendiary effect on Americans, many of whom believed it was
their country's destiny to liberate a downtrodden people from
Spain's occupying army.

When war was finally declared, the call to raise fighting forces
led to the creation of the First U.S. Volunteer Cavalry Regiment. With other volunteer and regular army units, the Rough
Riders willingly joined in the nation's first overseas conflict, but
the U.S. soon found itself not only undermanned but also ill-
equipped and untrained, especially for a campaign involving
highly coordinated land-sea operations. It was fortuitous that
the Spanish military was even less prepared.

In retrospect, sending soldiers to a tropical climate in the
summer months wearing wool uniforms was irresponsible.

This, coupled with the lack of a strategy for transporting men and equipment from Tampa, Florida, and the deplorable sanitary conditions aboard ships, as well as the fact that our artillery and regular infantry units were still equipped with weapons using black powder that exposed their position to enemy fire, constituted a national disgrace.

The lack of preparedness and questionable motivation for involvement can be argued in the comfort of hindsight. But the result was that the Spanish-American War marked the beginning of the United States as a world power. It was a popular conflict, especially among westerners; spirited men of ambition who relished their personal freedom and were fully aware of the benefits reaped from conquering their own frontier. It also turned out to be America's shortest war. The Cuban Campaign lasted only 113 days.

Even in that brief time, the Rough Rider experience produced the sort of human bonding that comes only from adversity, especially combat. It was something each man could carry with him the rest of his life, something worth remembering. Just as they had eagerly enlisted in 1898, Billy and most of his comrades embraced, with equal enthusiasm, the idea of Rough Rider reunions.

In August of 1898, a few weeks before the unit disbanded, Theodore Roosevelt told guests at his Long Island home that he would "talk about the regiment forever." He kept his word. The following year, while governor of New York, he traveled to Las Vegas, New Mexico Territory, for the Rough Riders' first reunion, held on the June 24 anniversary of the Battle of Las Guasimas. Centrally located and having produced the largest contingent of volunteers for the regiment, New Mexico was considered the logical location, and the small town of Las Vegas eventually won the honor of hosting the reunion after a spirited intrastate competition with both Albuquerque and Santa Fe.

Nationally known newspaper editor William Allen White of the *Emporia (Kans.) Gazette*, accompanied Roosevelt on the train trip west, reporting on the enormous crowds that greeted him at stops between Albany, New York, and Las Vegas. The Rough Riders arrived from all over the country, many taking advantage of special fares offered by the Santa Fe Railway. One man, who could not afford rail fare, arrived in a mule-drawn wagon after he and his new bride spent ten days plodding along dusty roads. "I've had a hell of a time getting here," he declared, "but I ain't sorry that we started."

A rainstorm on opening day ruined most of the city's elaborate outdoor decorations but did not dampen the enthusiasm of over six hundred Rough Rider officers and troopers gathered at that first reunion. The men, who had been victors in Cuba only a year before, renewed friendships and recounted experiences during the three-day celebration that included parades, band concerts, and a rodeo. Above all, the men wanted their wives, sweethearts, and families to meet their beloved Colonel Roosevelt, who, in typically gregarious form, spent thirty-six hours among them talking virtually nonstop.

All attendees, including Roosevelt, camped out in the city's Lincoln Park where the veterans met to formally organize the "National Association of Roosevelt Rough Riders," following through on plans first made when the regiment shipped out of Tampa Bay for Cuba. In addition to socializing, the former Rough Riders pledged to help each other find employment and get out of difficulties. They also proposed to meet yearly until none of their number remained.[5]

Oklahoma City hosted the second Rough Rider reunion. The 1900 event was held during the July 4 holiday and featured the glamorous Rough Riders' Ball, one of the town's most famous social affairs. Although Billy was far away, performing in Rome, New York, his heart was surely in Oklahoma City when guest of honor Theodore Roosevelt arrived there by special train late on July 2. He was greeted by an enthusiastic crowd of twenty thousand people, a remarkable turnout considering the population of Oklahoma City was then only about ten thousand. Surrounded by former members of his regiment, Roosevelt walked to the Lee Hotel for a reception. At the time,

it was the city's only such establishment with electrically operated elevators.

Shortly after midnight, Roosevelt made his entrance at the
lavishly decorated Rough Riders' Ball. The location chosen for
the affair was nothing short of genius. With neither air condi-
tioning nor fans to cool a building suitable for an event of that
magnitude, organizers decided the Street and Reed Furniture
Store, then under construction at 214 West Main, would be
ideal. Although the building did have a roof, the siding had not
been put on, allowing a natural cooling breeze to help sweep
away the hot, sticky summer night's air.

Tents scattered about the building's spacious floor accented
the military theme, and yards of bright red, white, and blue
bunting underscored the patriotic tone. An estimated five hundred men and women from the "Twin Territories" and nearby
states attended that night. The dances alternated between a
two-step and a waltz, and each had a name associated with the
famed regiment such as: Cuba Libre, Hard Tack and Bacon;
Roosevelt's Pride, Boot and Saddles, and San Juan Hill.

The next morning a military parade advanced along the city's
downtown streets. A detachment of the Eighth Regular Cavalry
led the procession, and behind them came Roosevelt, mounted
on a magnificent black charger. Riding with him were several
staff officers in full dress uniform, and following on foot, came
over one hundred Rough Riders, most wearing remnants of
their old uniforms. The parade also featured approximately
three hundred Civil War veterans from both sides, and scores of
Indians and cowboys.[6]

The march ended at the fairgrounds where a huge crowd
cheered when Roosevelt finally ascended the bandstand. Territorial governor Cassius Barnes and Oklahoma City mayor Lee
Van Winkle were scheduled to speak first, but the anxious audience would have none of it. They subjected the governor and
mayor to noisy calls for "Teddy" and cries of "cut it out."
Finally, when the Rough Riders' commander stepped to the
podium, the crowd hushed as he enunciated each word, clear

Teddy Roosevelt, on a black stallion, leads the Rough Rider contingent along
Main Street near Broadway during the July 2, 1900, Rough Rider reunion
parade in Oklahoma City. Courtesy of the John Dunning Collection.

and crisp like a hammer stroke: "You are bone of my bone and
blood of my blood, and to some of your sons I am bound by
some of the closest ties that can bind one man to another. . . . I
hope to come down here often and next time I come I hope to
see you a state."[7]

The Rough Riders held their next reunion at San Antonio in
early April 1905, an affair timed to celebrate Roosevelt's presidency. There is no record, but Billy almost certainly supported
Roosevelt in his run against Alton B. Parker, the Democratic

The 1900 Oklahoma City
reunion pin. Courtesy of the
John Dunning Collection.

candidate. The election of 1904 had afforded him the first
opportunity to win the office in his own right, after having
advanced to it from the vice presidency when William McKinley was assassinated in 1901. Less than a month after his inau-
guration, Roosevelt headed to Texas aboard a special train, a
cross-country journey westward that, again, brought out large
crowds along the way.

He made a point of stopping in Muskogee, Oklahoma,
which in 1898 had served as the recruiting headquarters for
Rough Rider volunteers from Indian Territory.

Now, in 1905, at the same depot in Muskogee where troops
had departed, fifteen thousand people had gathered to greet
President Roosevelt, and among them was Alice M. Robertson, destined to become Oklahoma's first congresswoman.
Only a few weeks earlier, Roosevelt had appointed her post-

mistress of Muskogee, giving her the distinction of being the first woman to hold that position in a first-class post office. Alice Robertson had known the president for several years, and she had close ties to the Indian Territory Rough Riders.

Born at Tullahassee Mission in the Creek Nation, she had taught at Indian schools in Oklahoma and Pennsylvania, and later worked for the Indian Commission. She became acquainted with the president when the two were involved in philanthropic work on behalf of Indian reservations. During the recruitment of Troops L and M, Alice Robertson took a personal interest in some of the Indian soldiers who had been her pupils.[8] She sent Roosevelt letters of introduction for them, and when they returned from Cuba, she continued looking after their welfare. When the regiment disbanded, Roosevelt wrote to ask her if any of the Rough Riders needed financial help. She replied:

> Some of the boys are poor, and in one or two cases they seemed to me really needy, but they all said no. More than once I saw tears come to their eyes at thought of your care for them, as I told them of your letter. Did you hear any echoes of our Indian war-hoops over your election? They were pretty loud.[9]

From Muskogee, Roosevelt's train followed the Katy rail line to Sherman, Grayson County, Texas, where newspapers reported that a crowd of thirty-five thousand had come by "buggy, horse, and special trains" from as far as 175 miles to see him. The train stopped long enough for Roosevelt to head a parade led by a unit of Rough Riders. The presidential party rode along the banner-decked streets in "nine handsome carriages," passing between lines of Union and Confederate Civil War veterans.[10]

Undoubtedly, the reunion in Texas was the first of the many that Billy attended. Since his discharge from the Rough Riders, he had either been on the road with the Buffalo Bill show or tied to the responsibilities of running a ranch. In 1905, he and

Mollie had moved into their new home near Ripley, Oklahoma, and now had the freedom to travel on their own.

Upon reaching San Antonio, Roosevelt and his men camped at the fairgrounds where they had trained seven years earlier. Following a parade through the heart of town, Teddy gave a rousing speech in front of the Alamo, and on April 8 he departed to Frederick, Oklahoma, for a few days' hunting before returning to Washington.[11]

The president could have hunted in Texas just as well, but he preferred that Oklahoma get the attention because he wanted the territory to become a state during his administration. Then, too, he was enticed to go because of stories about a young homesteader near Frederick named John "Jack" Abernathy, who caught coyotes alive with his bare hands.

The hunt was arranged in an area known as the "Big Pasture," a 480,000-acre parcel of land along the Red River that had been set aside for common use by the Kiowas and Comanches during the 1901 land opening. Denton County, Texas, cattle barons Burk Burnett and W. T. Waggoner, leased the range from the Indians and organized the "prairie wolf" or coyote hunt for the president. The party included Captain Bill McDonald of the Texas Rangers, Comanche Chief Quanah Parker, Jack Abernathy, several ex-Rough Riders, and some cowhands and ranchers.[12]

Roosevelt and the other hunters operated from a base camp along Deep Red Creek. The hunt, or "coursing," as he termed it, required several teams of greyhounds to run the prairie wolves to exhaustion so they could be killed or captured alive by the hunters who followed on horseback. As simple as it sounded, the terrain that stretched west toward southern Oklahoma's Wichita Mountains contained many hazards for a hunter on horseback. For one, the countryside was full of prairie dog holes and infested by rattlesnakes, and, galloping along at full speed, a rider depended on the instinct and quickness of his cow pony. The snakes he tried to kill with quirts or ropes before the greyhounds could attack them, usually with fatal results for the dogs.

The hunting party seemed impressed with the down-to-earth president. The *Oklahoma State Capital* reported that "Teddy likes 'chuck' too, eats beef and beans like the rest of cowboys."[13] Shortly after returning to Washington, Roosevelt designated the Wichita Forest, west of the "Big Pasture," the nation's first federal game preserve,[14] and in 1907 he signed the proclamation making Oklahoma the forty-sixth state.

Although there were no official reunions for several years after 1905, the Rough Riders took every opportunity for informal get-togethers. In 1907, the Arizona contingent had special reason to celebrate in Prescott at the unveiling of an imposing bronze statue of a mounted Rough Rider. Although dedicated to the memory of Captain William Owen "Buckey" O'Neill, the former Yavapai County sheriff and mayor of Prescott who died at San Juan Hill, the monument honored all First U.S. Volunteer Cavalrymen. It was reminiscent of Remington's sculpture of a bucking horse, which Billy's regiment had presented to Colonel Roosevelt at the end of the war.

In 1905, the Arizona Territorial legislature had given Solon Hannibal Borglum, the brother of Gutzon Borglum, who would later carve Mount Rushmore, a commission and partial funding to cast the monument. Sizeable private contributions, including one "generous" sum from President Roosevelt, finally made it a reality. On July 3, 1907, a long parade wound through the streets of Prescott where businesses and homes were draped in red, white, and blue. Marching behind a regular army cavalry troop from nearby Fort Whipple came scores of Rough Riders, Civil War veterans, and prominent Arizonans, including Governor Joseph H. Kibbey. When everyone had gathered on the lawn at the courthouse square, Maurice O'Neill, Buckey's son, pulled the ropes that dropped a canvas shroud displaying Borglum's masterpiece in public for the first time. The figure of a cavalryman seated on a straining, up-rearing horse is still considered one of the finest equestrian statues in the United States.[15]

Billy had returned to show business in the spring of 1907, so he probably was not among the Rough Riders who met at Prescott, or at the reunion of all Oklahoma Spanish-American War veterans in Guthrie that July 4 holiday. Former Rough Rider and territorial governor Frank Frantz presided over the event, which included war veterans from other states.[16] Only thirteen years earlier, Frantz had been part owner of a hardware store in Medford, Oklahoma. He returned to his home state of Illinois to earn a college degree and was working as a clerk for an Arizona mining firm when the Spanish-American War began. Frantz volunteered for the Arizona Rough Riders, and took command of Troop A when Captain "Buckey" O'Neill was killed at San Juan Hill. In the face of deadly Spanish fire, he rallied the men, carried the troop's colors to the crest of the hill, and planted them in the ruins of an enemy fortification. The act earned him a promotion and the lasting admiration of Roosevelt. After the war, Frantz settled in Enid, Oklahoma, where, in 1902, Roosevelt appointed him postmaster. Two years later he became the Osage Indian agent at Pawhuska, and in 1906, Roosevelt appointed Frantz the last territorial governor of Oklahoma.[17]

Billy certainly was present when Rough Rider veterans held their fifth national reunion in New York City in late June 1910. Many of the veterans traveled on a chartered train from St. Louis. The transportation had been arranged by Rough Rider Association president Charles Hunter of Enid, who planned for the New York assemblage to be part of a welcome-home ceremony for Roosevelt, who was returning from a fifteen-month tour of Africa and Western Europe.[18]

On June 18, a crowd estimated at one million people greeted the ex-president in Battery Park after he transferred from an ocean liner to the Revenue Cutter's *Manhattan* (the Revenue Cutter Service later became the U.S. Coast Guard). After viewing a Hudson River water parade of more than one hundred vessels, the Rough Riders joined in a procession up Broadway. It was following this homecoming and subsequent Rough Rider reunion that Billy rode out to Southampton, Long Island, where he won the national bronc riding championship.

The New York welcoming event also marked the beginning of Roosevelt's attempt to revitalize his political career by joining with progressive reformers against hard-line Republican conservatives. This so-called "progressive conservative movement" in the Republican Party soon gave rise to a new political party popularly known as the Bull Moose Party.[19]

In 1912, the Rough Riders' gathering, centered again on Roosevelt's political aspirations, this time in Chicago at the Republican National Convention. Colonel "Teddy" was a full-fledged presidential candidate once more and had already won most of the country's primary elections but faced a nomination fight against incumbent president William Howard Taft. Roosevelt had previously supported his fellow Republican but later opposed Taft for his lack of progressiveness on such issues as conservation, anti-trust legislation, and women's suffrage.

For the Chicago trip, Roosevelt supporters chartered a Rock Island Railway train dubbed the "Roosevelt Special." Consisting of several Pullman, dining, and observation cars, it departed El Reno, Oklahoma, on the afternoon of June 15, making stops in Kingfisher, Hennessey, Enid, Jefferson, and Medford as it steamed toward an afternoon arrival in Chicago the following day. Oklahoma's Taft supporters boarded a Frisco Railroad train that began the same journey north from Lawton via Oklahoma City and the northeastern part of the state.[20]

The Chicago convention resulted in a bruising political battle that deeply split the Republican Party. Although Taft outmaneuvered Roosevelt to eventually win the nomination, Roosevelt continued to campaign on the Progressive Party ticket. He visited Oklahoma City on September 24, 1912, making a speech at the fairgrounds, where the crowd included many of his comrades, but as faithfully as the Rough Riders and their families supported him, they were far too few to turn the vote in his favor.[21] Although Roosevelt outpolled Taft in the general election that year, both men lost by a wide margin to Democrat Woodrow Wilson.[22]

Through the years, Roosevelt's men liked to say that their colonel "was always as ready to listen to a private as to a major-general." The "colonel" proved them right, always taking pleasure in personal visits and correspondence from his former troopers. After the war, they demonstrated their loyalty with their political support and the firm belief that he could do almost anything, including getting them out of any predicament. One classic letter he received from a Rough Rider read:

> Dere Kunnel: I'm in trouble an' I want you to git me out of jale right away. Kunnel, I shot a lady in the eye. The lady is my wife's sister. But Kunnel I wasn't shootin' at the lady a-tall, I was shootin' at my wife.[23]

On July 6, 1919, seven years after his unsuccessful run for president as an independent candidate, Theodore Roosevelt died in his sleep at Sagamore Hill. It would be another eighty-two years, long after Billy McGinty and the other Rough Riders were gone, before the United States government would finally rectify what had been one of his biggest disappointments. The entire military chain of command in Cuba, including four army generals, had not only witnessed his gallantry at San Juan Hill, they had recommended him for a congressional Medal of Honor, but the award was denied by the War Department, apparently because of Roosevelt's outspokenness.

Even though all the American field commanders in Cuba had wanted to get their troops out of the malaria-infested tropics when the fighting was done, career officers were reluctant to complain openly. Roosevelt, not being regular army, articulated, to both Washington and the press, the need to "bring the troops home" quickly. His complaints embarrassed Secretary of War Russell Alger and President William McKinley, who never forgave his candor.

For decades after his death, Roosevelt's family and ardent supporters persisted in the notion that he deserved the award. Finally, on October 22, 1998, Congress approved awarding the medal for his "conspicuous gallantry" on San Juan Hill, more than one hundred years earlier.[24]

Sixteen years passed after their informal reunion at the Chicago Republican convention before the Rough Riders gathered again. Billy was among those in attendance at the Roosevelt Hotel in Hollywood, California, on June 24, 1928.[25] Not only was the hotel chosen for the name, its location in the movie capital was calculated to help generate public interest in the new Hollywood film *The Rough Riders*. The picture, directed by Victor Fleming, was a fictional account of the unit's experiences in Cuba. It had premiered at New York's George M. Cohan Theatre in March of 1927, when a *Times* review proclaimed it "excellent fun" and "bully entertainment." Although, the star-studded cast included Noah Beery, Charles Farrell, and Mary Astor, *The Rough Riders* was a victim of bad timing. Silent films were floundering at the box office that year because of the release of the musical *The Jazz Singer*, the first full-length movie with some "synchronized dialogue." Al Jolson's smash hit heralded the era of "talkies," setting the standards for all pictures to come and outdating everything else.[26]

Joining Billy and the others at the 1928 reunion was his friend and fellow Troop K soldier Lewis Maverick, a technical consultant on the Rough Rider film who had helped direct some of the battle scenes. Lewis was the grandson of the early Texas cattleman Samuel A. Maverick, who had allowed his cattle to roam unbranded. The term "maverick" was eventually used to mean any calf without a brand or earmark that was not following its mother. In open range country, "mavericks" could be legally branded by any cattle outfit that found them.[27]

Between 1928 and 1948, the regiment met only four times: at Chicago, Oklahoma City, and twice in Los Angeles. When Rough Riders assembled for their fifty-year reunion in 1948, 65 of the 107 surviving members of the regiment traveled to

Prescott, Arizona. The location was chosen in honor of home-town hero "Buckey" O'Neill, whose eighty-four-year-old widow, Pauline, attended as a special guest.

A photographic production portraying the regiment's glory days highlighted the reunion. Rough Rider and former war correspondent Edwin Emerson of New York had used over three hundred old photographs of their training and war service to produce a slide show. Although unable to attend due to illness, Emerson entrusted the presentation to Jesse Langdon, whose presence gave seventy-seven-year-old Billy McGinty a chance to tell his comrades how he had won a bet on Langdon over forty-eight years earlier.

Billy recalled that in 1900 the Buffalo Bill show played in Fargo, North Dakota, Langdon's hometown. Only thirteen riders were available that day, and because thirteen was an unlucky number, Buffalo Bill wanted one more. Langdon, who had joined the show for the first time, was tabbed as the four-teenth man in the riding act. Billy said that the other cowboys figured he was just a local guy with no experience, so they all bet against him when it came time for the bronc riding act. Billy had served with Langdon in Troop K, and knowing that the lanky youngster was an exceptional horseman, he encouraged the others to bet against him, especially when the "new man" drew the second-toughest bronc in the show.

The other riders put up a hatful of money, which Billy matched with his own wager. Then everyone gathered to watch Langdon "bite the dust." Those cowboys, Billy remembered, slowly lost their confidence when the bronc, "Blue Dog," bucked, pitched, and sunfished with Langdon in full control. Finally, riding him to a standstill, Langdon spurred "Blue Dog" to one end of the arena, then reached down, caught the bridle and yanked, throwing the horse to the ground as he easily slid from the saddle, landed on his feet, and waved to the cheering crowd. The cowboys stood slack-jawed as Billy held his hand out to collect on the bet.[28]

In 1949, fifty years after their first reunion in Las Vegas, New Mexico, the Rough Riders returned to that city. The same men who had once rushed to glory moved more slowly, and although only about fifty of their number attended the gathering, the cowboy volunteers of '98 seemed never to lack for patriotism, zeal, and wit.

Frank C. Brito, a Yaqui Indian serving with New Mexico troopers, told the others about the day he enlisted: "My father sent for us and said, 'Did you know the United States is at war with Spain?' When we answered no, he said, 'I want you boys to go to Silver City and enlist and fight for your country.' Them days, you did what your father told you to do."[29]

Ben H. Colbert of Tulsa, who volunteered at San Antonio and was assigned to Troop F those many years ago, was also there. The part-blooded Choctaw-Chickasaw Indian was the great-grandson of Levi Colbert, who commanded a regiment of Chickasaw Indians in the 1815 Battle of New Orleans. Following his service in Cuba, Roosevelt appointed Colbert a deputy U.S. marshal for the southern district of Indian Territory, and later he worked for the *Tulsa World* and the Spartan Aircraft Company. The distinguished, nattily dressed, seventy-six-year-old Colbert jested to his comrades that he had "gone through the war as a buck private and was never reduced."[30]

For the next several years, the dwindling number of Rough Riders met fairly often. Beginning in 1952, they decided Las Vegas, New Mexico, would be the permanent home for the National Association of Rough Riders, voting to hold all subsequent reunions there "to the last man." Billy, then vice-president of the association, assumed his usual role as regimental standard-bearer, carrying the colors while riding at the head of the parade that had become an annual tradition.

Only twenty-five Rough Riders made it to the 1952 affair. In addition to Billy, there were seven Oklahoma enlistees.[31] From Troop D came Theodore Folk and Ed Loughmiller, boy-hood friends who had grown up in Oklahoma City. The

Billy, left, and fellow Rough Rider Jesse Langdon lead the reunion parade in Las Vegas, New Mexico, in 1952. Langdon would be the Rough Riders' "last man." CSCPA Collection.

Czechoslovakian-born Folk was a nineteen-year-old grocery store employee when he joined, and Loughmiller had been working as a cowboy.[32] Other Troop D members were James T. Brown and Starr Wetmore, both from Newkirk, Oklahoma, and soldiers in Company I of the Oklahoma militia when they volunteered.[33]

James E. McGuire and George W. Wilkins, who served in Indian Territory's Troop L, also made the trip to Las Vegas that year, as did Ed Culver, a former cowboy from Vian, Indian Territory, who had been part of the advance guard during the heavy fighting at Las Guasimas.[34] Culver had been close friends with New Yorker Hamilton Fish, a sergeant in L Troop. When Fish was fatally hit by an enemy bullet, it passed through his body and struck Culver, lodging near his heart. Immobilized and barely conscious, he was left for dead on the battlefield, and by the time he was found and taken to a field hospital, he had already been listed as killed in action. Days later, Muskogee

Roosevelt's Roughriders and Cowboys Reunion at Las Vegas, New Mexico August 1, 2, 3, 1952

Back row. Tuttle, Prentice, Folk, Loughmiller, Wilkens, McGuire, Hamner, Lisk, Roberts, Crimmins, Wetmore, Brown, Langdon.
Front Row. Murray, Culver, Shaw, Gibson, Brumley, Yost, Denny, Brito, McGinty, Love, Hall, and Wyncoop.

Barely two dozen of the Rough Riders still living attended the 1952 reunion. CSCPA Collection.

newspapers had declared, "Ed Culver killed at Las Guasimas." The mistake was not discovered until after he was transferred to a hospital in the states, where he was eventually located by Judge John R. Thomas, who was visiting wounded soldiers from the troop he had helped to organize.[35]

Thirty former Rough Riders showed up for the 1953 reunion in Las Vegas. During the traditional storytelling that marked those affairs, Billy lamented not only their decreasing number but also the fact that, except for a very few, more than seven hundred members of the regiment left behind in Tampa in 1898 had never attended reunions. "They never come," Billy said sadly. "They felt so damn bad about it we never see them out here. It's too bad there just wasn't enough room."[36]

In 1954, after serving as vice president of the association for nine years, Billy was elected the organization's "president for life." For the next two summers, Billy, Mollie, and one of their sons or grandchildren made the drive from Ripley to Las

Billy leads the way for the Rough Riders' rodeo parade during the 1955 reunion in Las Vegas, New Mexico. Courtesy of City of Las Vegas Museum and Rough Rider Memorial Collection.

Vegas, but 1956 was Mollie's last reunion.[37] The following May, Mollie, aged seventy-two, passed away at the couple's home in Ripley. She was buried in the old Ingalls Cemetery, where her parents and other family members had been interred.[38]

Fourteen Rough Riders attended the Las Vegas reunion in 1957,[39] and when the sixtieth anniversary of the Spanish-American War rolled around in 1958, only six of the forty-four Rough Riders known to be living at that time attended the New Mexico gathering, including the durable Ben Colbert of Tulsa. That was the year Billy turned eighty-seven, and he and D Troop's Starr Wetmore of Arkansas City, who was eighty-five, drove their own car to Las Vegas to be with their four aging buddies.[40]

Before joining the Rough Riders, Wetmore had played trumpet in the town band of Newkirk, Oklahoma Territory, so he was selected the troop's bugler. Wetmore was wounded in fighting prior to the siege of Santiago, and after several weeks of not hearing from him, his family and friends feared he was dead. When they made inquiries about their son, the Wetmores were surprised to receive a telegram signed by President McKinley stating that he was recuperating from his wounds in New York. Upon returning home, Wetmore worked in real estate and construction, and later opened the Starr Theatre in Arkansas City, Kansas. Always passionate about the Rough Rider Association and his military service, Wetmore, in 1956, presented his battle-worn bugle, which sounded the last charge up San Juan Hill, to the U.S. Naval Academy in the name of his grandson, then a midshipman.[41]

In 1959, thirty-five Rough Riders were still living at reunion time, but only five managed to make it to Las Vegas. Billy's oldest son, Delmar, nicknamed "Red," and his wife Bessie, accompanied him, helping to boost him onto his horse for the parade. In addition to Billy, the 1959 reunion program listed seven other Oklahoma volunteers as still living.[42]

By 1960, the number of surviving Rough Riders had decreased to only twenty-eight. Billy and five others made the annual jaunt to New Mexico that summer, but it turned out to be Billy's last reunion. The following year, on May 6, 1961, Dr. George Hamner, a veteran of Troop F and the eighty-seven-year-old vice president of the Rough Riders Association, wrote a letter to Billy, who then lived with his son Jack in Ponca City, Oklahoma. Hamner reminisced about a particular moonlight night in Cuba sixty-two years earlier when the feisty McGinty and Clarence Wright sneaked out of camp to take in the sights of Santiago and how, on their way back, Billy rode his pony into an old French mansion that was occupied by some troopers. Hamner said that he'd never forget, "your asking Ray Clark [F trooper] to take your picture by the flash of your six-gun."[43]

Billy and Mollie McGinty, mid-1950s. CSCPA Collection.

Billy did not have the chance to answer the letter. Two weeks later, on May 21, the intrepid, wiry little bronc rider who charged up San Juan Hill with Roosevelt and lived out the largest part of his life in the little town of Ripley on the banks of the Cimarron, died at the age of ninety.[44]

Three or four of the still-living Rough Riders met in Las Vegas during the next few years. On the seventy-fifth anniversary of the Cuban campaign in 1973, only three authentic Rough Rider veterans were still alive, and two died that same year. The oldest survivor, George Hamner of Bay Pines, Florida, was ninety-nine when he passed away on February 6, 1973. The New Mexico volunteer had seen action at Las Guasimas, Kettle Hill, and San Juan Hill. After Cuba, Hamner earned a medical degree and served with the American Expeditionary Force in World War I. On April 22, 1973, ninety-six-

Billy McGinty in the late
1950s. Courtesy of the
Oklahoma Historical
Society.

year-old Frank C. Brito, the Yaqui Indian from Las Cruces, New Mexico, died in an El Paso, Texas, nursing home. Brito had been in Troop H, one of the four Rough Rider units left behind in Tampa. He had returned to military service with a National Guard infantry outfit in 1916 when rebel Mexican soldiers under Francisco "Pancho" Villa raided New Mexico.

Jesse D. Langdon of Fargo, North Dakota, and many other places during his long life, died on June 28, 1975, at a veteran's hospital at Castle Point, New York. Billy's Troop K comrade and fellow performer in the Buffalo Bill show had joined the Rough Riders at age sixteen. During his ninety-six plus years, he had worked as a veterinarian, builder, mechanical engineer, and inventor. Langdon was the only one to attend the last two "reunions" at Las Vegas in 1967 and 1968. He was the "last man."[45]

In the mid-1950s, when the National Cowboy Hall of Fame and Western Heritage Museum in Oklahoma City was still in its formative years, Billy's name was boosted for nomination but it was ruled that eligible inductees must be deceased. The paperwork was placed on file then, but revived in 1994. Six years later, on April 1, 2000, the nomination process was completed.

Billy McGinty, cowboy, Rough Rider, Wild West and cowboy band showman, and bronc riding champion, a little guy who always stood tall in the saddle, was named to the "Hall of Great Westerners," the museum's highest honor.[46]

Notes

1. INTO ACTION WITH THE ROUGH RIDERS

1. Virgil Carrington Jones, *Roosevelt's Rough Riders* (1971), 14–15; Dale L. Walker, *The Boys of '98* (1998), 57–60. The initial board of inquiry report of March 21, 1898, claimed the *Maine* had been destroyed by the "explosion of a submarine mine," but seventy-eight years later, in 1976, Rear Admiral Hyman G. Rickover and other navy specialists concluded there was no evidence of an "external explosion," rather that it was heat from a coal bunker fire that touched off an adjacent ammunition magazine (Walker, 280).

2. John Alley, "Oklahoma in the Spanish-American War" *Chronicles of Oklahoma*, 20, no. 1 (March 1942): 45.

3. Theodore Roosevelt, *The Rough Riders* (1999), 1–14 ("three cavalry regiments," 6); Walker, *Boys of '98*, 78 (McKinley-Wood exchange, 78); Clifford P. Westermeir, *Who Rush to Glory* (1958), 69–70, 215, 231. The Second and Third Volunteer Cavalries were commanded by Colonels Jay L. Torrey and Melvin Grigsby, respectively. The Second waited out the Cuban campaign in camp at Jacksonville, Florida, and the Third languished at Chickamauga, Georgia (Westermeier, 8, 185, 201).

4. *Guthrie Daily Leader*, May 8, 1898; Ann Nelson, "Rough Riders," *Oklahoma Today* (May–June 1998 ["my opportunity," 6]).

5. J. Stanley Clark, "The Career of Judge Thomas," *Chronicles of Oklahoma* 52, no. 2 (Summer 1974): 172 ("175 picked men," "moving his bed"); Brad Agnew, "Wagoner, I. T.: Queen City of the Prairies," *Chronicles of Oklahoma* 64, no. 4 (Winter 1986): 35.

6. Clark, "Career of Judge Thomas."

7. Walker, *Boys of '98,* 144.

8. Jones, *Roosevelt's Rough Riders*, 27, 102, 310; *Guthrie Daily Leader*, May 15, 1898.

9. Jones, *Roosevelt's Rough Riders*, 34, 39; Roosevelt, *Rough Riders*, 17 ("could keep step," "no braver man").

10. Roosevelt, *Rough Riders*, 13.

11. Ibid., 33–38; Jones, *Roosevelt's Rough Riders*, 69–78; Dale L,. Walker, *Buckey O'Neill, The Story of a Rough Rider* (1983), 149–54 ("lunatic asylum," 149; "sea of sewage," 154).

12. *Columbia Encyclopedia*, 6th ed. (2005), *s.v.* "Marro Castle."

13. Jones, *Roosevelt's Rough Riders*, 86–89.

14. Roosevelt, *Rough Riders*, 44; Jones, *Roosevelt's Rough Riders*, 100; Walker, *Buckey O'Neill*, 156–57 ("transport captains acted").

15. Jones, *Roosevelt's Rough Riders*, 108–9; Roosevelt, *Rough Riders*, 14; Walker, *Buckey O'Neill*, 150–51, 160. "Fightin' Joe' Wheeler served briefly in the Philippines from 1899 to 1901, then returned home to retire. He passed away in Brooklyn in 1906 (Walker, *Boys of '98*, 278).

16. John Adair, Oklahoma Historical Society, Indian-Pioneer History Project Interview # 12806, January 24, 1938.

17. Jones, *Roosevelt's Rough Riders*, 294; Roosevelt, *Rough Riders*, 91.

18. Vertical file, Oklahoma Historical Society; Box-MU25, GDSWAC.

19. Roosevelt, *Rough Riders*, 13 ("best soldier"), 47, 48, 52, 58, 61; Jones, *Roosevelt's Rough Riders*, 24, 25, 27; Walker, *Boys of '98*, 179; Nelson, "Rough Riders." When word of Captain Capron's death reached Fort Sill, there was much sadness throughout the post, even among the Apache prisoners of war, who considered Capron a great friend. One Apache, Sam Haozous, named his newborn son Allyn Capron Haozous (Towana Spivey, director, Fort Sill Museum).

20. Walker, *Boys of '98*, 190; Jones, *Roosevelt's Rough Riders*, 160, 162.

2. THE PUSH TO SANTIAGO AND SAN JUAN HILL

1. Walker, *Boys of '98*, 199–204; Jones, *Roosevelt's Rough Riders*, 161, 165; *Brooklyn Star*, September 20, 1898.

2. Walker, *Boys of '98*, 210–12; Richard Harding Davis, *Notes of a War Correspondent* (1910), 94. Buckey O'Neill had once written a short story with an eerily prophetic passage: "Death was the black horse that came some day into every man's camp, and no matter when that day came a brave man should be booted and spurred and ready to ride him out" (Walker, *Buckey O'Neill*, 176).

3. Walker, *Boys of '98*, 212–22; Roosevelt, *Rough Riders*, 76; Richard Killblane, "Spanish-American War: Battle of San Juan Hill," *Military History* (June, 1998, 38–45); *Hennessey (Okla.) Clipper*, July 28, 1898; Arlington National Cemetary, "Jules Garesche Ord, First Lieutenant, United States Army," http://www.arlington_cemetery.net/julesgar.htm.

4. Roosevelt, *Rough Riders*, 98; Jones, *Roosevelt's Rough Riders*, 199.

5. Cherokee Strip Cowpunchers Association, private collection (hereafter CSCPA Collection), Albert F. Stehno, Billings, Okla.; Jones, *Roosevelt's Rough Riders*, 27, 114; *Kansas City Times*, November 11, 1967.

6. Roosevelt, *Rough Riders*, 94, 95 notes; *Stillwater Gazette*, July 21, 1898.

7. Jones, *Roosevelt's Rough Riders*, 39, 73; Roosevelt, *The Rough Riders*, 99.

8. Walker, *Boys of '98*, 242–44.

9. Jones, *Roosevelt's Rough Riders*, 125; Roosevelt, *Rough Riders*, 86 (quoted). Charles Johnson Post, the *New York Journal* artist and a private in the Seventy-first New York regiment said of the old Springfield Trapdoor: "With each discharge there burst forth a cloud of white smoke somewhat the size of a cow." He concluded that the rifle could "knock down two men, the one it hit and the one who fired it" (*Boys of '98*, 108).

10. Jones, *Roosevelt's Rough Riders*, 48, 220.

3. SURRENDER, OCCUPATION, AND HOMEWARD BOUND

1. Roosevelt, *Rough Riders*, 117.

2. Jones, *Roosevelt's Rough Riders*, 217.

3. Roosevelt, *Rough Riders*, 17, 67.

4. Ibid., 17.

5. Walker, *Boys of '98*, 109, 185–86.

6. Jones, *Roosevelt's Rough Riders*, 336; *Guthrie Daily Leader*, May 1, 1898.

7. Jones, *Roosevelt's Rough Riders*, 338.

8. Roosevelt, *Rough Riders*, 126 (quoted); Walker, *Boys of '98*, 276–77. In 1921, President Warren G. Harding appointed Wood governor-general of the Philippines. He died there in 1927, following surgery for a brain tumor.

9. Edwin Emerson Papers, International Affairs Collection, Georgetown University Library Collection, Washington, D.C.; Edwin Emerson file, City of Las Vegas, Rough Rider Memorial Collection (hereafter RRMC).

10. Jones, *Roosevelt's Rough Riders*, 255.

11. Walker, *Boys of '98*, 263.

12. Ibid., 264.

13. Ibid., 264–66.

4. FOOTLOOSE AND FREE

1. Walker, *Boys of '98*, 268. According to historian Stewart Holbrook, William Rufus Shafter may have been "the most cruelly maligned general officer of courage, competence and patriotism in our history" (ibid., 277). He returned from Cuba with little personal glory to resume command of the army's Department of California. He retired in 1901 after forty years of continuous service, beginning as an enlistee in the Seventh Michigan Infantry in the Civil War. He died in Bakersfield, California, in 1906.

2. Edward Renehan, Jr., *The Lion's Pride, Theodore Roosevelt and His Family in Peace and War* (1998), 133–37, 232–39.

3. Roosevelt, *Rough Riders*, 138; Walker, *Boys of '98*, 105, 256, 268–70 (Roosevelt quoted, 269).

4. Jones, *Roosevelt's Rough Riders*, 26; Roosevelt, *Rough Riders*, 10, 11, 25, 92.

5. Cameron Winslow, "Cable Cutting at Cienfuegos (May 11, 1898)," *The Century* 57, no. 5 (March 1899).

5. THE BUFFALO BILL SHOW

1. Jones, *Roosevelt's Rough Riders*, 282–340; Walker, *Boys of '98*, 282.

2. North Dakota Cowboy Hall of Fame; Hank Johnston, *Death Valley Scotty: The Man and the Myth* (1972), 7.

3. R. L. Wilson, *Buffalo Bill's Wild West: An American Legend* (2004), 41, 46, 48, 56, 155; CSCPA Collection; William R. Everdell, *The Neighborhoods of Brooklyn* (2004).

4. Wilson, *Buffalo Bill's Wild West*, 49.

5. *New York Times*, March 30, 1899.

6. Robert W. Rydell and Rob Kroes, *Buffalo Bill in Bologna: The Americanization of the World, 1869–1922* (2005), 106.

7. Information from *Route Book for Buffalo Bill's Wild West, Season of 1900*, CSCPA Collection.

8. Nellie Snyder Yost, *Buffalo Bill: His Family, Friends, Fame, Failures and Fortunes* (1979), 147; Wilson, *Buffalo Bill's Wild West*, 142, 148–52, 249–52.

9. Robert K. DeArment, *Bat Masterson* (1979), 339–40.

10. Wilson, *Buffalo Bill's Wild West*, 78.

11. Joe Starita, *The Dull Knifes of Pine Ridge* (1995), 87, 136.

12. Interview with Gail Woerner, rodeo historian, May 14, 2006.

13. Jeanne Hubbard, Joyce Family Genealogy.

14. Wilson, *Buffalo Bill's Wild West*, 228–29, 236–37; Yost, *Buffalo Bill*, 290.

6. COWBOYS, CHARACTERS, AND SHOW SHENANIGANS

1. 1904 World's Fair Society, St. Louis, Missouri, "A Visit to the Pike," http://www.1904world'sfairsociety.org/.

2. Joseph H. Carter, *Never Met A Man I Didn't Like: The Life and Writings of Will Rogers* (1991) 19, 20.

3. Gail Woerner, *A Belly Full of Bedsprings, The History of Bronc Riding* (1998), 10; Mari Sandoz, *The Cattlemen from the Rio Grande across the Far Maria* (1958), 492.

4. Carter, *Never Met a Man I Didn't Like*, 42–44.

5. Johnston, *Death Valley Scotty*, 9, 12, 31–34, 37–42, 44, 47–48.

6. Ibid., 17–19.

7. *Guthrie Daily Leader*, September 8, 1913.

8. *New York Times,* May 2, 1900; Roosevelt, *Rough Riders,* 122.

9. *Prairie du Chien Courier Press,* August 23, 1900; May 31, 1972; CSCPA Collection ("Drunken deputy"; other quotes are from *Courier Press*).

10. Roosevelt, *Rough Riders,* 57; Robert K. DeArment, *Revenge* (2004), 44–45, 51, 81, 185.

7. BACK HOME IN OKLAHOMA

1. Box MU-25, Glenn D. Shirley Western Americana Collection (hereafter GDSWAC), Dickinson Research Center, National Cowboy & Western Heritage Museum, Oklahoma City. Billy's contract with the Buffalo Bill Company shows he was paid twenty dollars per week with a two-dollar-a-week bonus at the end of the season if he stayed the entire season.

2. Leslie McRill, "Old Ingalls: The Story of a Town That Will Not Die," *Chronicles of Oklahoma* 36, no. 4 (1958), 429–30.

3. Diary of Dr. Jacob H. Pickering, in the Billy Jay McGinty family, Glencoe, Oklahoma.

4. Box MU-25, GDSWAC.

5. Box MU-26, GDSWAC.

6. McRill, "Old Ingalls," 436.

7. Diary of Dr. Jacob H. Pickering.

8. Ibid.

9. Ibid.

10. Ibid.

11. Interview with Billy Jay McGinty, May 15, 2006; MU-25, GDSWAC. Dr. Pickering's diary was handed down by daughter Mollie to other descendants of the McGinty-Pickering marriage, and remains a valued piece of family as well as Oklahoma history.

12. Although the terms "Strip" and "Outlet" are sometimes used interchangeably, they, technically, denoted two different areas of land. In 1854 the southern boundary of Kansas was created at the 37th parallel, thereby taking in a 2.46-mile-wide strip of land previously assigned to the Cherokee tribe. This became the so-called Cherokee Strip. Following the War between the States, the Cherokees agreed by treaty to cede the land in trust to the United States to become a part of Kansas. The "Cherokee Outlet," meanwhile, took in about 226 miles in length, was fifty-eight miles wide, and after 1866 was all in Indian Territory. In reality, the Cherokee Strip Livestock Association, made up of cattlemen, leased the lands of the Cherokee Outlet for grazing purposes from the Cherokee tribe. The Outlet was opened by land run to white settlement in 1893 (George Rainey, *The Cherokee Strip* [1933], 1, 36–41).

13. Glenn L. Eyler and Billy McGinty, *Old West* (1937), 65–69.

14. Box MU-25, GDSWAC. Billy was sworn in as a Day County Deputy Sheriff on July 28, 1902.

15. John W. Morris, *Ghost Towns of Oklahoma* (1977), 94, 95. The town of Grand became the county seat of Day County in 1893. In 1907, Day County ceased to exist and the new county of Ellis was formed, which took in part of Woodward County. That portion of old Day County south of the Canadian River then became part of Roger Mills County.

16. Box MU-25, GDSWAC.

17. Leslie McRill, "The Story of an Oklahoma Cowboy," *Chronicles of Oklahoma* 34, no. 4 (1956), 436–37; Billy Jay McGinty interview.

18. Billy McGinty, unpublished manuscript, 1939; Glenn Shirley, *Red Yesterdays* (1977), 121.

19. Box-MU-25, GDSWAC.

20. *New York Times*, June 25, 1910.

21. Santa Barbara Historical Society Museum, Santa Barbara. John Edward Borein grew up in the California cow town of San Leandro and began sketching at age five. He became a well-known watercolorist, painter, and newspaper illustrator, and counted Frederic Remington, Theodore Roosevelt, Charles Russell, Will Rogers, and Hollywood's Leo Carillo among his closest friends. In 1907, he opened a studio in New York, and later moved to Santa Barbara, California, where he continued his career until his death in 1945.

22. McGinty, unpublished manuscript; Glenn Shirley, *Pawnee Bill* (1958), 148–53; *McCook (Nebr.) Daily Gazette*, April 18, 2005.

23. *New York Times*, July 3, 1910.

24. MU-25, GDSWAC.

25. McGinty, unpublished manuscript; Shirley, "Bad Broncs and Bullets."

26. Glenn Shirley, *West of Hell's Fringe* (1990), 426–27; McRill, "Old Ingalls": 1437.

27. Shirley, *West of Hell's Fringe*. 428–29.

28. Bob L. Blackburn, *Images of Oklahoma* (1990), 67; George H. Shirk, *Oklahoma Place Names* (1987). Fulkerson was renamed for Aaron Drumright, the owner of the land on which the townsite was laid out in 1913.

29. MU-22, GDSWAC.

30. Billy Jay McGinty interview.

31. Carla and Dale Chlouber, "Young Jack McGinty's Trip through the West," *Payne County Historical Review* 13 (Fall 1993), 11–13. Ghost Hollow, about two miles northeast of Ripley, is a sometimes marshy area with a scattering of old oaks, cottonwoods, and sycamores. Local legend is that an innocent man was hanged there in 1887, and the next day the bark mysteriously fell off the tree. For years, people claimed that at full moon the tree glowed an eerie white color.

32. MU-22, GDSWAC.

33. Letter from Roy Chessmore, City of Las Vegas, Rough Rider Memorial Collection, July 24, 1995.

34. Chessmore letter, RRMC; *Ripley Record*, February 1, 1923.

35. *Stillwater Gazette*, September 11, 1931; MU-25, GDSWAC.

36. Leslie A. McRill, "Music in Oklahoma by the Billy McGinty Cowboy Band," *Chronicles of Oklahoma* 38, no. 1 (Spring 1960): 66.

37. Carla Chlouber, "Otto Gray and His Oklahoma Cowboys, The Country's First Commercial Western Band," *Chronicles of Oklahoma* 75, no. 4 (Winter 1997–98): 357–58.

38. Gene Allen, *Voices on the Wind, Early Radio in Oklahoma* (1993), 11, 13–14, 19–20, 26, 31.

39. Quoted in McRill, "Music in Oklahoma," 67.

40. *Ripley Record*, May 14, 1925; MU-22, GDSWAC ("mike fright" quote). Other early band members named by Billy included Johnny Bennett, Roy Munday, and Bert Bevins (Box MU-24, GDSWAC).

41. McRill, "Music in Oklahoma," 72.

42. On September 13, 1927, KVOO radio officially moved to Tulsa. W. G. Skelly acquired full ownership of the station in 1928. By then, financial difficulties had already begun to plague Rollestone, and two years later the thirty-six-year-old financier committed suicide (Allen, *Voices on the Wind*, 34, 35).

43. Box MU-22, GDSWAC.

44. McRill, "Music in Oklahoma," 72, 73.

45. *Coshocton (Ohio) Tribune*, April 17, 1926.

46. *Tulsa Tribune*, June 1, 1926.

47. *Stillwater Gazette*, February 28; September 29, 1926.

48. Robert Shelton and Bert Goldblatt, *The Country Music Story* (1971), 152–56.

49. Shirley, *"Bad Broncs and Bullets."*

8. TO THE LAST MAN

1. *Daily Oklahoman*, May 2, 1932.

2. *Stillwater Gazette*, September 26, 1924; *Tulsa World*, September 18, 1932; CSCPA Collection.

3. CSCPA Collection. Rolla Goodnight later took a home on the Logan–Lincoln County line where the town of Goodnight, Oklahoma, was founded. It has since become a ghost town.

4. Ibid.

5. Walker, *Boys of '98*, 272; Westermeir, *Who Rush to Glory*, 253–56 ("hell of a time," 255).

6. Pendleton Woods, "The Rough Riders' Reunion," *The Motorist*, Oklahoma Division of the American Automobile Association magazine (July–August 1977), 8–10.

7. Angelo Scott, *The Story of Oklahoma City* (1939), 174–76.

8. Box MU-25, GDSWAC; Grant Foreman, "The Hon. Alice M. Robertson," *Chronicles of Oklahoma* 10, no. 1 (March 1932), 15.

9. Roosevelt, *Rough Riders*, 16, 142.

10. Quoted from State of Texas Historical Marker.

11. *Frederick Enterprise*, April 7, 1905.

12. "Catch-'em-alive-Jack," as he was known, earned his nickname by accident when a stray wolf once attacked his dogs. Jack jumped into the middle of the brawl and thrust a gloved hand into the wolf's mouth, luckily far enough back to avoid the canine teeth. Pinning the wolf with his knees, he grabbed both upper and lower jaws with his free hand and then clamped them closed as he worked his other hand out the side of its mouth. He then wired its jaws shut. Abernathy had turned this unusual feat into a profitable business, living on wolf bounties before becoming a successful rancher and deputy sheriff in southwestern Oklahoma. (Jim Fulbright, *W. D. "Bill" Fossett, Pioneer and Peace Officer* [2002], 196–99).

During the 1905 hunt along the Red River, President Roosevelt witnessed Abernathy live up to his name when, after a run of several miles, he caught up to a fatigued wolf and "headed him," as if cutting a cow from a herd. Roosevelt rode up just in time to see Jack jump from his horse and spring atop the animal. He wrote: "I was not twenty yards distant at the time, and as I leaped off the horse, he was sitting placidly on the live wolf, his hands between its jaws, the greyhound standing beside him, and his horse standing by as placid as he was. . . . It was as remarkable a feat of the kind as I have ever seen." (Theodore Roosevelt, *Outdoor Pastimes of an American Hunter* [1905], 113–14).

13. *Oklahoma State Capital,* April 12, 1905.

14. Department of the Interior, "U.S. Fish and Wildlife Service, Wichita Mountains Wildlife Refuge," Early Administrative History, http://www.fws.gov/southwest/refuges/wichitamountains/pdf_files/BRIEFPKG.pdf

15. Walker, *Buckey O'Neill*, xi, 185, 186.

16. *Daily Oklahoman*, July 5, 1907.

17. Vertical file, Oklahoma Historical Society.

18. Ibid.; *Daily Oklahoman*, April 19, May 5, 1910.

19. Renehan, *Lion's Pride*, 44.

20. *Daily Oklahoman,* June 9, 1912.

21. Ibid., July 3, 1920.

22. Renehan, *Lion's Pride*, 45.

23. Box MU-26 GDSWAC; Roosevelt, *Rough Riders*, 143.

24. Renehan, *Lion's Pride*, 31–32; *Newsday,* October 22, 1998.

25. Misc. files, RRMC.

26. *New York Times*, March 16, 1927.

27. CSCPA Collection.

28. *New York Times,* June 24, 1948; *Prescott Evening Courier*, June 25, 1948. Pauline O'Neill married Buckey's younger brother, Eugene Brady O'Neill, in 1901. He died tragically, by apparent suicide, in Los Angeles in 1917. She lived to be ninety-six (Walker, Buckey O'Neill, 183).

29. Westermeir, *Who Rush to Glory,* 258.

30. *Daily Oklahoman*, December 18, 1921, December 10, 1960; Box 1, folder 100.22, RRMC; Westermeir, *Who Rush to Glory,* 258.

31. Misc. filcs, RRMC.

32. Box 4, folder 100.89, RRMC.

33. *Newkirk Democrat*, May 4, 1898.

34. Misc. files, RRMC.

35. Jones, *Roosevelt's Rough Riders*, 114, 127–28; *New York Times,* July 29, 1898; Maggie Culver Fry, *Sunrise over Red Man's Land* (1981), 68–73.

36. *Tulsa Tribune*, May 22, 1961; *Albuquerque Tribune*, August 10, 1953.

37. McRill, "Oklahoma Cowboy," 439.

38. *Stillwater Gazette*, May 9, 1957. Mollie McGinty died on May 6, 1957.

39. *Daily Oklahoman*, August 12, 1957.

40. Ibid., July 13, 1958.

41. *Ponca City Daily Courier*, September 15, 1898; *Daily Oklahoman* July 13, 1958; Box 6, folder 100.52, Rough Rider Memorial Collection; Newkirk Community Museum; Box MU-24, GDSWAC.

42. 1959 Rough Rider Reunion Program, RRMC.

43. Box MU-26, GDSWAC.

44. *The New Mexican*, August 7, 1960; *Tulsa Tribune*, May 22, 1961.

45. Walker, *The Boys of '98*, 280–82.

46. *Stillwater News-Press*, February 27, 1994; April 11, 2000.

Bibliography

ARCHIVAL COLLECTIONS

Cherokee Strip Cowpunchers Association. Private collection of Albert F. Stehno, Billings, Oklahoma.

City of Las Vegas Museum, Las Vegas, New Mexico. Rough Rider Memorial Collection.

Dickinson Research Center, National Cowboy & Western Heritage Museum, Oklahoma City. Glenn D. Shirley Western Americana Collection.

Georgetown University Library, Washington, D.C. Edwin Emerson Papers, International Affairs Collection.

Billy Jay McGinty family collection, Glencoe, Oklahoma. Diary, Jacob H. Pickering.

Newkirk Community Museum, Newkirk, Oklahoma. Spanish-American War Collection.

1904 World's Fair Society, St. Louis, Missouri. "A Visit to the Pike," http://www.1904world'sfairsociety.org/.

North Dakota Cowboy Hall of Fame. Center for Western Heritage, Medora, North Dakota.

Oklahoma Historical Society, Oklahoma City, Oklahoma. John Adair, Indian-Pioneer History Project Interview #12806.

―――. Vertical files.

Santa Barbara Historical Society Museum, Santa Barbara, California. Edward Borein Collection.

BOOKS

Allen, Gene. *Voices on the Wind, Early Radio in Oklahoma*. Oklahoma City: Western Heritage Books, 1993.

Blackburn, Bob L. *Images of Oklahoma*. Oklahoma City: Oklahoma Historical Society, 1990.

Carter, Joseph H. *Never Met A Man I Didn't Like: The Life and Writings of Will Rogers*. New York: Avon Books, 1991.

Davis, Richard Harding. *Notes of a War Correspondent*. New York: Charles Scribner's Sons, 1910.

DeArment, Robert K. *Bat Masterson*. Norman: University of Oklahoma Press, 1979.

———. *Revenge*. Lafayette, Indiana: Scarletmask, 2004.

Everdell, William R. *The Neighborhoods of Brooklyn*. New Haven: Yale University Press, 2004.

Fry, Maggie Culver. *Sunrise over Red Man's Land*. Claremore, Okla.: Claremore College Press, 1981.

Fulbright, Jim. *Trails to Old Pond Creek*. Goodlettsville, Tenn.: Mid-South Publications, 2005.

———. *W. D. "Bill" Fossett, Pioneer and Peace Officer*. Goodlettsville, Tenn.: Mid-South Publications, 2002.

Hill, Luther. *History of the State of Oklahoma: Vol. II*. New York: Lewis Publishing Company, 1908.

Johnston, Hank. *Death Valley Scotty: The Man and the Myth*. Yosemite, Calif.: Flying Spur Press, 1972.

Jones, Virgil Carrington. *Roosevelt's Rough Riders*. Garden City, New York: Doubleday & Company, 1971.

McGinty, Billy, and Glenn L. Eyler. *The Old West*. Ripley, Okla.: Ripley Review Publishers, 1937.

Marshall, Edward. *The Story of the Rough Riders*. New York: G. W. Dillingham Co., 1899.

Morris, John W. *Ghost Towns of Oklahoma*. Norman: University of Oklahoma Press, 1977.

Rainey, George. *The Cherokee Strip*. Guthrie, Okla.: Co-Operative Publishing Co., 1933.

Renehan, Edward J., Jr. *The Lion's Pride, Theodore Roosevelt and His Family in Peace and War*. New York: Oxford University Press, 1998.

Roosevelt, Theodore. *Outdoor Pastimes of an American Hunter*. New York: Charles Scribner & Sons, 1905.

———. *The Rough Riders*. New York: Charles Scribner's Sons, 1899; Modern Library Edition, 1999.

Rydell, Robert W., and Rob Kroes. *Buffalo Bill in Bologna: The Americanization of the World, 1869–1922*. Chicago: University of Chicago Press, 2005.

Sandoz, Mari. *The Cattlemen from the Rio Grande across the Far Marias*. New York: Hastings House, 1958.

Scott, Angelo C. *The Story of Oklahoma City*. Oklahoma City: Times-Journal Publishing Company, 1939.

Shelton, Robert, and Bert Goldblatt. *The Country Music Story*. Secaucus, N.J.: Castle Books, 1971.

Shirk, George H. *Oklahoma Place Names*. Norman: University of Oklahoma Press, 1987.

Shirley, Glenn, *Pawnee Bill: A Biography of Major Gordon W. Lillie*. Albuquerque: University of New Mexico Press, 1958. Repr., Lincoln: University of Nebraska Press, 1958.

———. *Red Yesterdays*. Wichita Falls, Texas: Nortex Press, 1977.

———. *West of Hell's Fringe: Crime, Criminals, and the Federal Peace Officer in Oklahoma Territory, 1889–1907*. Norman: University of Oklahoma Press, 1990.

Starita, Joe. *"The Dull Knifes of Pine Ridge: A Lakota Odyssey*. New York: G. P. Putnam's Sons, 1995.

Thoburn, Joseph B. *A Standard History of Oklahoma,* Vol. V. Chicago & New York: American Historical Society, 1916.

Walker, Dale L . *Buckey O'Neill, The Story of a Rough Rider.* Tucson: University of Arizona Press, 1983.

———. *The Boys of '98*. New York: Tom Doherty and Associates, Inc., 1998.

Wellman, Paul. *A Dynasty of Western Outlaws*. Garden City, N.Y.: Doubleday & Company, 1961.

Westermeir, Clifford P. *Who Rush to Glory*. Caldwell, Idaho: Caxton Printers, 1958

Wilson, R. L. *Buffalo Bill's Wild West: An American Legend*. Edition, N.J.: Chartwell Books, 2004.

Woerner, Gail. *A Belly Full of Bedsprings, The History of Bronc Riding*. Austin: Eakin Press, 1998.

Yost, Nellie Snyder. *Buffalo Bill: His Family, Friends, Fame, Failures and Fortunes*. Chicago: Swallow Press, 1979.

PERIODICALS

Agnew, Brad. "Wagoner, I.T.: Queen City of the Prairies," *Chronicles of Oklahoma* 64, no. 4 (Winter 1986).

Alley, John. "Oklahoma in the Spanish-American War" *Chronicles of Oklahoma* 20, no. 1 (March 1942).

Chlouber, Carla and Dale. "Young Jack McGinty's Trip through the West." *Payne County Historical Review* 13 (Fall 1993).

Chlouber, Carla. "Otto Gray and His Oklahoma Cowboys, The Country's First Commercial Western Band." *Chronicles of Oklahoma* 75, no. 4 (Winter 1997–98).

Clark, J. Stanley. "The Career of Judge Thomas." *Chronicles of Oklahoma* 52, no. 2 (Summer 1974).

Foreman, Grant. "The Hon. Alice M. Robertson." *Chronicles of Oklahoma* 10, no. 1 (March 1932).

Killblane, Richard. "Spanish-American War: Battle of San Juan Hill." *Military History* (June 1998).

McRill, Leslie A. "Music in Oklahoma by the Billy McGinty Cowboy Band." *Chronicles of Oklahoma* 38, no. 1 (Spring 1960).

———. "Old Ingalls: The Story of a Town That Will Not Die." *Chronicles of Oklahoma* 36, no. 4 (Winter 1958).

———. "The Story of an Oklahoma Cowboy." *Chronicles of Oklahoma* 34, no. 4 (Winter 1956).

Nelson, Ann. "Rough Riders." *Oklahoma Today* (May–June 1998).

Shirley, Glenn. "Bad Broncs and Bullets." *Western Magazine* (February 1970).

Winslow, Lieutenant Cameron. "Cable-Cutting at Cienfuegos: May 11, 1898." *The Century* 57, no. 5 (March 1899).

Woods, Pendleton. "The Rough Riders' Reunion." *The Motorist*, Oklahoma Division of the American Automobile Association magazine (July–August 1977).

NEWSPAPERS

Albuquerque Tribune
Brooklyn Star
Coshocton (Ohio) Tribune
Daily Oklahoman
El Reno (Okla.) News
Frederick (Okla.) Enterprise
Guthrie (Okla.) Daily Leader
Hennessey (Okla.) Clipper
Kansas City Times
McCook (Nebr.) Daily Gazette
Newkirk (Okla.) Democrat
Las Vegas (N.Mex.) New Mexican
Newsday (Long Island, N.Y.)
New York Times
Oklahoma State Capital
Ponca City (Okla.) Courier
Prairie du Chien (Wis.) Courier
Prescott (Ariz.) Evening Courier
Ripley (Okla.) Record
Stillwater (Okla.) Gazette
Stillwater (Okla.) News-Press
Tulsa Tribune
Tulsa World

Index